THE NICOLE RODRIGUEZ STORY

PUNISH HER

SISTER OF A LEGEND

NICOLE RODRIGUEZ

This story is dedicated in memory of my big brother and only brother

Christopher Lee Rios

a.k.a BIG PUN

(November 10, 1971 through February 7, 2000)

I HOPE YOU ARE PROUD OF ME

1 LOVE YOU and S.I.P

INTRODUCTION

"I would like to begin by saying that the purpose of my book is not intended to hurt or offend anyone. Although many will be affected about what I will share with the world- I cannot sugar coat the reality of my life —unfortunately the truth hurts, and I will not lie in fear of hurting you. In advance I apologize but it took me ten years to write my story and now I am confident enough to tell it"

Everyone in life has gone thru something-some stories may be worse than mine but mine was too much for me to manage. As a child up until I became a teen, I was put down a lot, craved affection, and love, and often compared to my sister's beauty. I never shown stability- I never was told about the birds and the bees. I wasnt raised or nurtured in a happy or healthy household. I only learned "survival of the fittest" to make it thru my life. I strongly believe will are all products of our environment and therefore I eventually became disillusioned with my own. The cycle never broke for me and my life growing up impacted me in such a way that I grew to experience much of what I witnessed. I grow up to deal with abusiveness and unstable relationships. Dysfunction I was accustomed too and it was all I attracted in life. My life was me, my mom, and my brother Chris-this is all I knew. Despite our dysfunctional upbringing, my brother and I prove that we can become something great regardless of our circumstances.

STORY

My name is Nicole "Nicky" Rodriguez born on February 25th, 1977, at 10:12pm. My mother gave birth at her place of employment, Albert Einstein College of Medicine in Bronx NY The proud parents of me were my mother Gail Simpson and my father Thomas Rodriguez. My mother was a divorced former aspiring model and actress. My dad was a military boy from a religious and strict household. Together they could have conquered all but their mutual acts of poor judgment soon take them on a ride to rock bottom.

My mother was the oldest of three siblings. She had two younger brothers from a separate father. My grandmother's favorite son was her youngest named Joseph. And the oldest son Luis was the stepfather's favorite. My mom was no one's favorite. My mom shared with me that she was the victim of verbal, physical abuse. My grandmother would tell her "You ain't shit, you never going to be shit." She would go as far as to tell her, "I hated you from the first time I laid eyes on you and the best part of you ran down my legs after I had you."

My grandmother was a "santera" and often involved my mother in her rituals. Not that it was a terrible thing to be, but my grandmother used her beliefs to overpower those around her. She would bathe my mother in blood. She would cut off the heads of chickens and drip the blood over my mom in the bathtub. My grandmother would put all the parts of the mutilated chicken in a sac and make my mother take the chicken parts and bury them in the park.

My mom witnessed a lot of physical fights between her mother and step father Luis DeLaTejera. My grandmother was always attacking her husband because she always accused him of cheating. My mom described her mother as a "Narcissist" who believed the world revolved around her. Narcissistic personality disorder is a condition in which is excessively preoccupied with issues of personal adequacy, power, and prestige. For control or attention, she would go as far as pop pills and stick her head in the oven and inhale the fumes whenever she got in a fight with her husband.

While going through this, my mom was also dealing with not having a relationship with her father. My grandmother got pregnant to my mom around the age of eighteen from a handsome educated young man named Donald B Simpson. He was born in Canada and was of Indian descent. Both of his parents were born in the British West Indies, Jamaica. His family was very wealthy, and they did not approve of his relationship with my grandmother. They felt my grandmother was of lower class. He left her and went on to school at M.I.T for engineering.

My mother strongly blames my grandmother for driving him away by turning him off with the constant drama for money. She craved that fatherly affection that she was not getting from her mother. My mom said her mother never kissed, hugged, or said I love you. She was only good to my mom when people where around. Growing up with her mother, my mom was miserable and would spend hours sitting in her windowsill writing poems and stories. One time my mom wrote a biography, and her teacher became alarmed when she read the personal things my mom wrote in it. The school called my grandmother in and question her about what my mom wrote.

My mom did not see her father until the age of fourteen in court for child support. Her mother showed up with one legal aid lawyer and her father showed up with seven lawyers. This was the first time my mother and her father saw each other, and they stared and each other for a very long time. They looked identical to one another. He left her a fund for fifty thousand dollars that she could collect when she turned eighteen

My grandmother was able to get his address from court papers then gave it to my mother.

My mom went to his home and the doorman told her "His wife just left". A few minutes later her father came down and walked up to her outside the building. Then he gave her back her picture she gave him in court of herself. He told her " I don't ever want to hear from you or your mother again, don't look for me".

My mother saw him again in court a few years later when she was seventeen. On this day, my grandmother argued that my mother was not emotionally stable to handle the trust fund money and asked that she be awarded the fifty thousand dollars. She convinced the courts and was granted power over the money. My grandmother spent all the money on furnishing her apartment, buying her sons nice things, but only bought my mom a quilt set out of it.

Although her stepfather worked, the majority of the household income came from her child support. In addition, residual income came from my mother's modeling gigs, commercial skits and acting as an extra in a movie. She did a skit for a coca cola commercial and graced the front cover of" Tan Magazine" 1965 edition. In addition, she played as an extra in the movie "Up the Down Staircase and was offered an acting role in a soap opera called " The Nurses'.

As for my dad. his parents were born in Puerto Rico and were Pentecostal during his childhood years. His parents later split and divorce due to his father's affair with a young girl. This young girl was my grandmother's friend and bible study student. My father's dad was thirty-two and his new young mistress was only sixteen years of age. My grandfather and his newfound love both become Jehovah witness and my grandfather's demeanor began to change into a strict and cold man.

After witnessing his mother suffer from depression because of the affair and her several attempts of suicide, it really took a toll on my father. He later joins the Navy and then Army and was honorably discharged from both. My dad joined the military to get away and this is what introduced him to drugs. Heroine helped him deal with Vietnam and till this day he suffers from Post-Traumatic Stress Disorder (PTSD).

After a visit back home from the navy, he came home to encounter a seduction by his new and young stepmother. On top of that, he had to call a woman stepmom who was closer to his age than his fathers and later makes a pass at him. She would come in the bathroom when he showered and massage him and touch on him until one day it tempts my dad to sleep with her. This is a huge a secret till this day my grandfather still does not know about-but now he will.

Before I came along, my mom already had two children from her first marriage to David Rios. My brother Christopher and my sister Penelope (raised by my grandmother). My mom gave my sister to my grandmother when she was around seven years old. The only sibling to grow up at home with my mother and brother Chris was me. My mother said she gave my sister to my mom because my grandmother was always calling and crying that she was lonely. This left my life only to involve me, my mom, and my brother. It was us three that will later go thru all the storms together.

My mom met my dad when he was the neighborhood mail carrier. Coincidently, they both lived in the same building. It was a building across the street from Roberto Clement Park that faced over the Hudson River. My mother was living there with my brother on the sixth floor under a government funded assisted program for single mothers. My father lived with his friend on the seventeenth floor. Soon after, I was conceived and born into a life of misery. A life where I felt punished for all the mistakes my parents will soon make.

As a brief introduction to our life, I must begin by saying it was mostly an unhappy one.

Although I do not remember much before the age six, I remember before this time I was happy and seeing my family happy and close during that time. I remember many family parties and holiday get together. Our family parties and holidays lasted the whole weekend long. Friday night with music and dance and end with cards or dominoes then start again Saturday night and all over again till it ended on Sunday afternoon. As all the adults danced, all us kids played and watched them get drunk and make fools at themselves.

It was so much fun listening to Salsa at its best in the late 70s beginning of 80s and watching our parents spin on the dance floor. Then after wards they switch it up to disco and did the hustle all night. Now I must say, my family sure knew how to dances their behinds off. Since I was not born yet to tell, I leaned on my mother for support in filling in the details before my time and when I was too young to remember.

Before my premature birth at 7lbs at 7 months of pregnancy, my mother had placenta previa. I almost died at birth and had to spend several weeks in NICU. On the day I was brought home, my mother told mc my brother was excited to see me. She said my brother Chris rushed home from school and said, "Where is she??" He runs to my crib and stares at me threw the crib bars. One of the first questions he asked her was "why is she so hairy." Then my mom put me in his arms to hold- creating a bond that would last us his lifetime. Chris loved me and became very overprotective of me from the start.

Although my birth was happy news to some, my maternal grand-mother was not happy of the idea of a nigger granddaughter from my mom's nigger husband (a name she often called us repeatedly throughout the years to come). During an intense argument with my parents, my grandma purposely sprayed roach spray in my face and eyes when I was a few weeks old. When she sprayed that in my eyes my dad became very angry and nearly killed my grandmother.

My dad picked my grandma in the air and threatened to throw her off her eleventh

floor terrace or balcony some may call it. As he held her in the air, a neighbor watching from a lower-level floor screamed "put her down" "Don't do it". Eventually he put her down but he used to say he should have thrown her because she made everyone's life miserable. My grandmother whom us grandchildren called "Abuela" hated my father because to her he was "scum of the earth" and "a nigger." He was Puerto Rican with dry hair so to her he was straight up Black.

My mom told me that little over year before I was born, she took my brother who was five all the time to visit her cousin and friend. My brother stood downstairs at Manhattan Municipal Park with her best friend Carmen daughter Yvette. On a dare to climb a wall that surrounded the park, my big brother climbed up to the roof of a structure being built-he climbed until he was four stories high. At this point, he lost his balance and fell over; he landed on a pile of bricks. He broke his leg his arm and his jaw. This is the same fall that later will be the answer to his prayers.

When the security guard called upstairs, my mom ran down thirty-two floors, she said she thought she was faster than the elevator. When she saw him lying on the ground, she was in grief. The first words he said to her were "don't worry mom, don't cry I'm alright". She said his leg was mangled and distorted, so was his arm and face. She told me she never overcame the guilty feelings because she blamed herself for a very long time. Reason is while he was falling, she was upstairs smoking weed with her cousin's wife.

When my mom and Chris's dad broke up a year before my birth-Chris was still hurt over it and began to act up and get into lots of trouble. When I was a year old, my brother jumps off the roof of a daycare center and broke his arm again. This daycare was down the street from us, and it was closed-Chris had no business being there. My mom said he was a handful even when he was a toddler to age 5 was very hyper. He ran the teachers crazy at daycare and school. He was diagnosed with hyperactivity, and he was put on retalin.

My mom stopped giving it to him because it had a negative effect on him. It was hard to get mad at him because he was so funny.

My mother knew Chris would be a handful from the start because when he came out the womb, he had both his fists folded like a boxer. My brother began acting out by wetting his bed till age 7 (this is around the time that my mom met my dad). My mom said my brother was born 11-10-71, 8 pounds and twelve ounces. He was twenty inches long. When he came with those two clinched fists. She knew he was ready for the world. She said he was the most beautiful baby boy she ever saw. He was always happy and smiling.

He started walking on his 1 st birthday. He started preschool/daycare at Davidson daycare. Here he drove the teachers "ragged" my mother stated. My mom says he was extremely hyper and would jump from the top of the bunk bed to the floor. He would play superman and jump of the top of the hamper.

Now back in 1981-1982, I was about six years old, and Chris was twelve. Chris would always make front of my weight because at the time I was the chubby one and he was the slim one. One time I was crossing the street without looking both ways when we lived on Marion Avenue near Fordham road in the Bronx. He told me to be careful because if they hit me, they going to sue me for denting their car.

One time my mother and I were home alone. While I was in the living room watching "Bugs Bunny", I heard my mom yell loud "Nicky, Get out the house!" She runs out the room, pushes me out the door, and tells me to run. We run 5 floors down and when I look back, I see a man chasing behind us with a knife. My mother screams to me "hurry up" and because I was chubby and couldn't run that fast, she pick me up and threw me down the last few flights of stairs (she definitely was my hero

"SUPERMOMMY". When we made it to the ground floor, we knocked on the super (landlord) door-she opened up but immediately shut the door in our face when she saw what was going on. Terrified we both stood with nowhere else to run in front of this door. The intruder caught up to us and just waved the knife in our faces-I then looked at him and smiled out of nervousness he then looks at me back and runs away.

I remember catching my parents having sex in our living room. This was traumatizing to me. I told my dad "get off my mommy!"-Then he yells at me with authority tone "go to your room!" Now that I think back, he should have said go back to the kitchen cause that's where my brother and I shared a bunk- I slept on top and he slept on bottom. Our bedroom was supposed to be the dining room area. My parents ended up walking to their bedroom naked holding hands- then I go to the same sofa and lay down to watch Chevy Chase movie "Shaggy".

I remember my mom had the habit of saying play dead whenever my brother got on her nerves or stressed her out. One time to teach her a lesson, Chris and I played dead and laid on the floor in front of the front door with ketchup all over us —and a butter knife laid next to us- we wanted to teach mom a lesson for always saying "play dead"- and it worked, when she walked through the door she started screaming she was hysterical thinking we were really dead. When she dropped to her knees beside us, she realized it was a joke when she smelled ketchup- she was so mad at us for playing that joke. Truth was, it really hurt my brother's feelings when she said to go play dead.

Chris was always acting up in school and I went with my mom for many teacher

parent conferences My mother had a challenging time handling my brother to the point she hit had to him. I remember one time she got so mad at him she hit him on the head with her high heel shoe. The heel cut his head and made him bleed. I saw in her face that she felt bad and afraid she hurt him worse than what she intended to do. Another time she put a lock in a sock and hit him with it. At first, I felt bad but Chris would always look at me and then we startcracking up- my mother got so mad.

My mother was so stressed with us kids and on top of that my brother's hyperactivity was making him hard to control. My mother she started smoking "Salem" cigarettes heavy. She would always tell me to put out the cigarette in the toilet then I would secretly smoke the "butt." that was left. Her smoking made me so curious to light a match myself that I snuck a pack of matches to her room and lit her brand-new red carpet on fire.

Unlike my brother, I was very quiet and shy. I was much calmer and never got into any trouble. Chris hated school but was extremely bright. I loved school and was academically a great student. Even when I felt sick, I never had to be woken up to go to school. I was always doing extra credit and loved learning new things. One thing we did share was our humor and love for laughter. Later, we learn we share another common love.

I remember my brother was always putting pillows over my face then he would fart on it. I hated that disgusting joke. I remember my brother and I were so greedy, especially me. Our mother would buy us both our own dozen box of Entenmanns chocolate frost donuts. Once, I sat and ate 11 out of the dozen back-to-back-I got so nauseous that I vomited all over the house, I was so greedy that I would lock myself in my room so I didn't have to share my food. Other times I would put my arm over my plate to guard it. My brother hated when I did this- especially because he loved having the last bite of everyone's food or be the first to crack open the soda because he like to hear the fizz.

I remember my mom told me the story about how when us kids were not home for the night- my mom and dad spent an alone night together. My mother made dinner for my dad. When my mom went to serve him, he grabbed her, tied her up and threw her in the closet. My mom goes along because she taught it was a kinky sex; tease game he was playing or roleplaying. He then threw the plate of food at her and pulled out his sword on her that he got from traveling in the military that hung in our living room wall. Now realizing this is no game, my mom gets nervous and yells to my dad "Tommy" what are you doing? It is me "Gail" when he realized what he done, he untied her and apologized. The post-traumatic stress disorder caused by Vietnam he suffers from till this day often caused him to have flashbacks or look at you as a Vietcong-as he thought my mom was.

After Fordham rd., we all move to Samson Avenue in the Bronx into the first floor of her friend her friends. private house. We only lived here for a few months. My parents were constantly fighting. During one of their altercations, my dad bent my mom's finger back (not purposely) and dislocated it. The happiest time here was when Alexander's was having a raffle to win the first cabbage patch ever. I was the winner, and her name was Neil Paula-because I was unable to pronounce it I would call her nail polish. I was about 6 years old I cherished her.

Winning something for the first time made me feel special-in other words important.

Around the years of 1983 and 1984, we all we moved to the Soundview area of the Bronx – the home of "Cozy Corner" where the real OGs are from. We moved to the first floor of a private house located at 544 commonwealth avenue (not 534 commonwealth as mentioned in "The legacy" documentary). Break dancing was popular this time and Chris was a huge fan. I remember dudes from the block would get the cardboard out and lay it down while true talent spun on their heads and battled each other while everyone was in a circle around them clapping their hands and dancing.

My mother enrolled me at P.S 69 just a few blocks up the hill. My favorite teacher here was Ms. Araujo. Mrs. Araujo use to get so mad at me when I would call her Mrs.

Carajo-a bad word that sounded like her name just to make everyone laugh in class. Besides going to a great school, our new home was the starting point to a roller coaster ride to rock bottom. I started to gain a lot of weight and eventually ended up being the heaviest and tallest girl in class at P.S 69.

By the fourth grade I was pushing 140lbs and wore about a 15/16 women's pants. My size fell in the category of what society calls today "Obese". I was picked on a lot by children in and outside of school. When I was picked on by other kids, I was always afraid to defend myself. My father always told me that it was not lady like for a girl to fight or talk with foul language. I did about anything to make these kids like me. I would buy them candy and even made a homemade swing from a rope and a pillow that I hung from a tree in front of my house. Now I was the coolest kid on the block who had lots of friends.

The main reason for my out-of-control weight gain was my mother's lack of control over our eating habits. On top of that, my mother had credit in about every store on the block from the Chinese Take Out down to the corner bodega. One thing I could say is whether it was a bag of nachos and a quarter juice with a pack of now or laters for desert —we ate. On the other hand, Part of my weight issues between the ages of eight and twelve came from my house-tohouse dinner visits to my friend's houses.

Although I already ate dinner at my house, I would lie to my friends mothers and say, " no I didn't eat yet." At times, I had three to four dinners in one night. The difficult part for me was developing last thing friendships. I spent most of my childhood moving a lot and changing schools consistently. Besides to eat, I also used visits to friend's homes to mentally fool myself by make believe that I was part of their family. The reason was I admired how happy and close they were. Life became very painful for me. I longed to have a happy stable family.

At home I witnessed lots of verbal and physical fights between my parents. I often played monkey in the middle between them both. Their constant fights both verbal and physical often entertainment everyone on our block. They would fight in their bedroom right by their window that faced the street- they had no shame-how embarrassing. When this would happen I would either lock myself in the room and blast my favorite song "we are the world" or swing on my homemade swing, or go sit across the street at bobs pizzeria. The pizza man would say "are your parents fighting again" damn I could not even eat in piece everywhere I go I was recognized as the daughter of Gail and Tommy. One time after leaving the pizza shop, I witnessed a man commit suicide by hanging himself with a TV cord from the fire escape. As soon as I was about to cross the street to go back home, this man landed right by my foot.

I remember my brother would get so stressed he would punch holes in his bedroom walls and eat the crumbs from the rocks in the wall. Part of the stress I think was he missed his father, wanted attention and affection. My brother and I sometimes escaped this environment by leaving the house, snap on each other for some laughs, or blast the radio in our room. Besides being very close growing up, my brother and I had something in common "MUSIC." Sometimes we would sing to each other around the house-we even would give each other ques from across the room. He would look at me from across the room or vice versa then start a line of a song then I'll comes out and due a verse like we were in a video. My mom looked at laugh and us like we were crazy. One of our favorite songs we would sing together and to each other as kids was " ebony and ivory" by Paul McCartney and Stevie Wonder. When we got older it was new editions "can u stand the rain". Overall,

Music was always the #1 escape for my brother

As retarded as a game it was, sometimes we would just play stupid games like lay upside down on the bed and continuously kick each other. Or he would hide me on the shelf of his bedroom closet and drive my parents crazy by having them think I was missing-and they running around saying "you seen Nicky" and Chris be like "NO" then when they left Chris and I start die laughing-then when they find me, they'd be so pissed. Although I never witnessed any type of physical abuse from my father towards my brother, my father was verbally authoritive towards Chris. This verbal authoritative way of discipline would be what society classifies as "verbal abuse." I do remember my dad always comparing Chris to me from school grades to who washes better dishes. My father was from the military and was harder on Chris because he was a boy. My father would make Chris do push-ups, flick him in the ear a lot or make him clean his room because it was dirty. I remember my brother would always say would you love me more if I were Black (referring to me)-the crazy thing is I felt the same but the other way around.

On a quest to prove his worthiness and show he is equally smart or better (in which he was). He would come up with outrageous words and tell my mom or mom/dad "I bet you I'm smarter than Nicky" "watch let me prove it" he will call me from my room to the living room where him, myself and the audience (my parents) all stood. Then he will put me on the spot and say "Nicky- what does monotonous mean? How do you spell it? Now mind you I am only 7 years old he is 13 years old. I will say, "1 don't know" then he'll say see I told you Nicky isn't smarter than me. My mother and father would say "come on Chris, now you expect her to know that she's only 7, these are big words and the only reason you know the answer is because you just looked it up

Chris was a naturally born genius who read the Encyclopedia and Dictionary religiously.

Speaking of religion, he even knew the bible beginning to end.

This is what made him the lyrical genius he was that later makes him a hip-hop legend.

Anyways, it appeared to me as if my brother were hurt when my mom or dad said that because I think he was disappointed because his intent to prove his worthiness got shut down and it seemed like she was defending the notion that I was smarter. Such feuds made me feel bad because to me he was my idol and personally I never felt smarter, and I never cared to hold that title. At times, this even caused Chris to resent me- at the same time he loved me to death. On a funnier note- I remember my mom loved wearing night gowns to bed but one breast would never stay in. Unknowingly, one breast would always pop out while she was cleaning or doing something around the house. My brother and me would laugh so hard-and say "ewwww ma put that away"

During the same time, I noticed my parents were acting strange and doing strange things like staying long periods of time alone or with friends in the bathroom. They would pass each other a little white piece of paper quick like I wouldn't see it or they would make up code language- You Should have heard How dumb they both sounded-I think they invented pig Latin.

My father was the first parent I caught using drugs- I was about 8yrs old. My father took my cousin and I to the park and I saw him by the slides sniffing cocaine- he used a spoon charm he had hanging from his chain. One time I took baby powder and dumped it all over the table and sniffed it. My parents said, "Where did you get that from" as young as I was I looked at my dad like "where do you think?" I got it from you! They immediately became defensive and denied having any influence for my actions and said "you never seen me do that".

If having one parent on drugs wasn't enough, I eventually catch my mom too. When I was about nine, I was walking to my moms room and as soon as I got to her door I caught her with a pen lid and that little white paper pouch I spoke about earlier in her hand about to take a sniff-

I was so disappointed in her cause I knew what it was- I just walked away and went to my room.

Thanks to the recent "Say No To Drugs Day" represented by Mcgruff and a speech from one of NY Police Officer at school, I knew exactly what drugs wcrc and that it was wrong to do.

My parents would pass drugs to each other —speak in secret codes as if it would throw me off-truth was I was very smart and observant-I knew exactly what was going on. They started getting sloppy and brave with their habit. They started taking me for the ride to by the drugs. My father would drive us to the Watson area of the Bronx or by Lexington Ave and park the car and have me sit in the car with my mother or at times alone while he went to go buy. One time my parents were so high they slept two days straight, Friday night to Sunday afternoon. They woke up to use the toilet maybe once and went back to bed.

I remember while they slept for those two days I went thru their video stash and found what I thought was a cartoon. When this video started playing I learned it was more than a cartoon. This cartoon turned out to be a cartoon pom of a pig having sex with the girls on the farm. I was disgusted and confused and never looked at cartoons the same after that. I remember my mom yelling threw her bedroom curtain-"Nicky what are doing?" I said "nothing, watching cartoons". Well technically I wasn't lying.

I remember a few weeks before I found my parents porn, I went with them to visit their friends at their home. They figured while they have fun and mingle, I can play with their sons whom were close to my age. As it became late in the night, my parents and married friends put all us children to bed. Us kids were nosy and decided to sneak a peak at what our parents were doing in the living room. When we come are the corner we saw all our parents watching porn together like it was nothing — as if it were a regular movie-it confused the hell out of us. When we returned home I did not know how to look at my parents.

Soon after, my favorite grandmother 'Gloria" (my dad's mom) died of breast cancer. She was the perfect grandmother and I was so heart broken over her death because we were extremely close. She kept me every summer in Puerto Rico, bought me anything I wanted and was my keeper of my favorite soundtrack record from Popeye the movie.

Before she died, Grandma Gloria would take out her dentures and remove her fake breast and chase me around the house. It was freaky and scared the crap out of me. Although not her biological grandchild, she treated Chris just as equal as me and brought him down to P.R too..

When she bought me something she bought him too. If she gave me money she'll give him too. Damn ,she even dressed us both alike on our way back to New York. She had me and Chris wear a red polo with beige dress shorts and a pair of puma sneakers. (Chris hated it).

Although summers were spent with Grandma Gloria in P.R, the following summer my mom signed us up for " The Fresh Air Fund". It was a government-founded program for lowincome families to take children from the city of New York port authority to stay with families in the country in Pennsylvania. I loved it because I stayed with a nice wealthy white couple that couldn't have children named Pauline and Craig Mullikan. They owned a steak house and were only able to adopt or foster children. On the other hand, my brother hated it because the couple that kept him would keep his clothes and underwear and give it to their son. My brother would come back to New York with no clothes.

Chris's world change when news came that his dad died in 1986. Chris shut down, my sister Pina dropped to the ground screaming. Chris began to act resentful towards because I had a dad around and he didn't. His father David was a nice man who treated me just like his own. Sometimes he picked me when he picked up my brother and sister for the weekends. After his father's death, Chris anger and aggressiveness issues worsened. Once he came home from IS 174 frantic because he knocked out a dude in front of the school unconscious. He though he killed the guy.

Eventually my parents constant fighting led them to split up around 1986. Right before the split-my parents had an argument and my mom accused my father of hitting her with a horsewhip my father had sitting against the wall behind the front door. My father love betting horses at Yonkers Raceway. The cops came and asked me did I see my father do that- I said "No". The cops left and told my father to leave and cool off- my mother was upset with me- she accused me of defending him and threw an ashtray at me but she missed- I really didn't see cause I was in my room when it all happened. When my father walked out to leave with his belongings my mother told him take your daughter with you-and he did.

Years later she tells me she just wanted to teach my dad a lesson- she new he would beg her to take me back after a few days-and he did. My dad kept me for two dayswe stood at a furnished room in Hunts Point where he shared rooms with other men who were in the same situation as him and worst. My dad eventually moved out the furnished apartment into an apartment he shared with a so-called friend. One day One time while visiting my dad he took me to visit my aunt Providencia in Hunts Point and here a mom was about to jump of roof of building with small child and commit suicide- my father had me turn my face as we try to walk away from the commission.

One weekend, my dad asked my mother could he have me for the. I remember he picked me up late at night and took me across town. I've Always been very observant, so unconsciously

I memorized exactly how to get from my house to where he was now living. I was only about 8 years old. I noticed at his house was a woman and her daughter. He introduced this woman as his roommate-that he was renting some space and slept in the living room. When I returned home, my mother asked me where I stayed I said at daddies friends house. My mom said what friend. I said an ugly lady who looked like Miss piggy. My mother asked me do I remember where they lived-I said "I think so"-she said take me their.

So we got in the car and off we went back across town to surprise my dad and his roommate. We finally made it their and my mother was shocked that I remembered how to get their-and my dad was too. My mom knocked on the door and the lady answers but my dad shuts the door on my mom foot. They start to struggle as my mom tries to make her way in- my dad did all he could to avoid it-it turned out my dad been seeing this woman for awhile and this was used as their official breakup.

Right after catching my parents, there split and my grandmother's death things started to go downhill fast. At this time my mom was working as an assistant for a local doctors office. One of the doctors became obsessed with my mother. My mother was in need of a car and my grandfather was selling one for $2500. This Doctor tried to win over my mothers with money so he gave my mom the money to buy it. When he saw his plan did not work, he showed up at our house one day with another man in a black trench coat and black gloves. At home were my mom, her friend, her two kids and I. The Doctor told my mother "Do you want me to kill you in front of your kids?" She said "No" —he said you better have my money by such an such date or I will kill you". I assume she did FAST cause he never came around again.

I did notice my mom sold all our furniture, toys, kitchen appliances, etc. . we were soon left with nothing. One day my mom was unable to pay the rent so the landlord Maria sent her youngest son who was the same age as me to collect rent payment. He had a speech impediment that caused him to stutter and strain to get a word out. When my mom answered the door to his knock, the boy slowly and stutterly tried to relay his mothers message to "ask for the rent money!" . His several attempts to get it caused my mom to get impatient then she yells out " What the Fuck You Want? Say it already"- that was so hilarious.

By the time Chris was around the age of fourteen, my mom felt Chris had a problem other than hyperactivity. Twice a week, He was seen my Dr. Faruk and Dr. Choudri a few blocks up the hill from us. But after three visits with him they refused to see him anymore and told my mom to be careful because Chris will either end up killed or he will kill somebody, he is gruesome, Chris has a need to control (in the future, this explains why he controlled his wife he had an illness, he needed help but never hot it).

These same doctors then referred him to Comprehensive at Albert Einstein and set him up with a counselor. It was here where he was evaluated and diagnosed as a potential sociopath. They concluded that Chris had no empathy or sympathy for others and no conscience. Some signs that were red flags to his doctors were that he killed cats and dogs. He use to throw them off the of buildings then laugh about it.

I noticed my mom was spending lots of time in the bathroom. When I would come in after her I noticed a strange smell that was unfamiliar to me. At times I saw pieces of aluminum foil in the bathroom around the house. I saw smoky foggy looking bottles with screw tops around the house and in her dresser draws. I saw little jars with white residue around. I noticed our home became a hang out for some strange new friends my mom was making. Now these same friends started accompanying my mom in the bathroom for long periods of time. Then my mom started spending less and less time at home and more on the streets. Sometimes she didn't come home at all. Sometimes I would sit on her window sill facing the avenue just crying my eyes out pleading and negotiating with God to please bring my mommy home safe and that I promised to be a good girl if he brings my mom home. Next thing my brother and I noticed was my mom started loosing weight drastically.

My mom allowed me to sleep over one of her friends houses who was heavy on drugs with her two kids one weekend. It was a "Welfare House" in Manhattan that housed other lowincome poverty stricken families. Everything was shared bathrooms, toilets, etc. it was a disgusting and filthy place. When I returned home after that weekend I started having trouble breathing a few days later and I began to turn white as a ghost. My mother got scared and walked me a few blocks up the hill to the Soundview medical clinic-immediately an ambulance was called and I was rushed to Jacobi HospitalI was suffering from a severe case of walking Pneumonia- doctors told my mom if she had waited any longer I would have died.

I spent two weeks in the hospital and I loved it because I was being cared and nurtured for by nurses-two things I lacked from home. When I got home from hospital from Pneumonia- Chris was so worried about me cause he thought I was dieing. He sat on his knees next to me on the sofa cried out "please Nicky don't die, " I promise Ill never pick on you again or hit you (the typical things siblings go thru)- I think he was being a little to hard on himself. Unlike what the doctors previously said about my brother, he showed me that he did care and had empathy for others. This totally contradicts what the doctors said about the fact he has no empathy or sympathy for others.

Next incident that took place was I walked over next door to the Chinese take out spot that my mom had credit at to buy some wonton soup-when I walked right back next door to my house with this greasy boiling hot soup I sat on my sofa with it to watch cartoons- few seconds later my white Maltese dog named Fifi jumped on my lap and the whole thing fell on my stomach and upper thighs area- I suffered 2nd degree burns. It was the most painful thing I ever experience it was worst than giving birth to my children. I remember I jumped up and robotically tore off my burning hot clothing —my mom ran out and didn't know what to do-so she put butter on it then toothpaste- I don't know where she got those tips from but it was the worst pain I ever felt till this day. Rather than take me to the emergency room and be accused of abuse or neglect by Children's and Families, she called her friend who was a nurse to care for my wounds.

As I got older I felt like I was being punished for my parents mistakes. Knowledge of my parents past caused disputes in my own personal life. Everyone I felt I could confide in and express myself too always threw it back in my face. Often I was told, "at least my mother wasn't a crack head", and this really hurt me each and every time. Friends would start rumors and say, "I saw your mom in Hunts Point selling her body for money." I was embarrassed and becoming resentful for the simple fact I have to deal with their consequences. I began to question my mom and asking her "mom is it true you was on the corner." She would say "Hell no! !! Where did you get that from?" I believe her because I don't feel she would have stooped that low-I hope not.

Same as me, Chris was having a difficult time dealing with witnessing my mother's drug abuse, his father leaving the family then his death, and my dad (his stepfather) being very hard on him. Chris became angry and self-destructive, punching holes in the walls and eating the rocks even more at our home. Soon after, Chris started getting into more and more trouble hanging in the streets got arrested, coming home with brand new clothes, and sneakers (Reebok classics with the gray line) Clark's shoes. He got arrested for the first time for running from the cops and was sent to the 21 st precinct near Story Avenue.

Overall, Chris enjoyed playing basketball earning the nickname "Goya Jordan" on the courts and later boxing. The injuries he sustained from his accident years prior started to resurface with discomfort walking. Doctor also noticed one knee was growing taller than the other. It was then doctor decided he would need another cast- Chris was like 14- Chris kept it on maybe two weeks but he couldn't take it no more- it was hot and itching like crazy. He took a pair of pliers, hammers and screwdriver and began to rip the cast apart as we both sat on the stoop in front of our house. My bother had to take some time off from school at IS 174 and get home tutoring while he rehabilitated from his injuries

My mom was unable to handle bills and rent anymore so we moved in with her mother. Chris stood in the streets, friends and girls houses. We did not stay for long because my mom and grandma were always fighting. I remember my grandma babysat me and kept shoving food down my mouth. She felt I was eating to slow so she kept force-feeding me. As I previously stated, my grandmother is a santera and her home scared the hell out of me. Her house was full of coconuts on the floors, turtle shells, Meringue, black dolls clothed with a hanky on their heads and beads all over their necks.

From here my mom and I moved out to my maternal aunt I will call Olga for book purposes (whom is deceased now) in the same area we were already living in. For money, my aunt babysat for parents who were single moms or struggling financially couples from the block. My aunt was very abusive toward the children she babysat (Ages months old to preschool).

My aunt played the sweet old lady who loved children in the building-but truth was these poor kids where dropped off to hell every morning. My aunt would stick children's heads in toilet, hit them; throw them around by their arm. I would watch all this as I sat on her red plastic covered loveseat that sat in the hallway near her front door entrance yet faced the living room. One time she was babysitting a 2-year-old African American girl, the poor baby told my aunt several times "I need to Potty" my aunt ignored her but the girl ended up wetting herself as she walked her own self to the bathroom. My aunt got up off her chair grabbed the girl and shoved her head in the toilet.

At the same time was a knock on the door, it was her daughter whom was a New York City Cop at the time. She was extremely upset over what she walked in on and said " If I see you do this again I will take you in myself". The reality was, this was her mother and it was not the first time she witnessed this behavior. On the otherhand, I can understand how difficult of a situation to be caught up in to have to turn in your own mother. As for me, I wanted to help these kids but I was only about a child myself and was afraid to speak up.

In retrospect, she was the rock for many of us back home in the Bronx- with her you would never have been homeless-she opened her home to you even if you did not have enough to feed herself she made sure we all ate- I often wondered how can someone so cruel be so good at the same time?? -I was actually closer to her than my own grandmother (her sister) that's why it hurts me to tell the world this but she was wrong when it came to those children she mistreated- I cannot overlook it like it never happened.

When it came to the family children (like myself) she did not touch us. I remember my aunt would give me money Sunday to buy her the "Sunday daily news" at the bodega in the corner. Instead, I would pocket the money and steal the paper from outside a house that their papers delivered. During this time, my brother's birthday came around. While I was on my way to the store to spend the money I been making from not really buying my aunts paper, I bumped into my brother in the corner. He asked me "did you buy me a card for my birthday" I said, "No I have no money", Chris says "you a liar"- "I know you got money". I said yeah but it's to buy candy." My brother says "candy is more important than me?"

For a little kid, he didn't understand that it was- I knew no better and did not understand what priorities were. My brother held this against me till for years. My brother started messing around with an older woman who lived upstairs from my aunt. She was the single moms of one of the kids my aunt babysat. I remember my brother would make out with her in the elevator as I stood their trying not to watch but the space was kind of tight in the elevator.

In order to cover room and board at my aunt's house, my mom would steal meat from the local supermarkets and sell it for money or give to my aunt to cook. Most often though, my mom would shoplift from local department stores and sell the stuff- she sold panties 10 for 10 bucks. Besides for room and board, my mother was also trying to hustle to support her habit. Often times, my mom brought me with her on her shoplifting sprees. She would have me stand next to her with a bag or her purse wide-open. Then she would throw items inside as I played her lookout. This was a job I never signed up for and I knew stealing was wrong.

It was kind of funny because as my mom would look around before she put the item in the bag, she would have this fake superficial yawn she would do every time. As if this really was going to distract or throw off the store associates. While my mother and I lived with aunt, my brother was still out in the streets hustling and fending for him. Around this time he met his junior high school sweetheart. Chris met her in the 8 th grade and if it weren't for Chris getting left back in the 7th grade, he would have never met her. Now he didn't have to daydream about Brooke shields anymore. I remember Chris came to visit my mom and he and I told me with excitement "wait till you meet my girl- she is so pretty she looks like you Nicky."

Wow!, did my big brother just call me pretty. Especially when I was deeply insecure about myself. Chris not only loved his new girlfriend but he loved her mom, brother and sister too. Her mom took Chris in and filled in that mother figure he was lacking from our own mom. One day Chris brought me to meet her and her family near Bronx River. Her mom cooked us some delicious steak and french-fries and I hit it off with her little brother.

Eventually, all these happy moments will start to come to an end- Chris girlfriend parents became concerned about the amount of time they were spending together. They felt my brother was a distraction and negative influence for their daughter. Chris was depressed when her father moved her up to Long Island to get away from him. For months they go thru the whole "I miss you" stage and finding-ways to sneak and see each other.

Around this same time, my mother started dating a man who owned his own business as a "CPA." He promised my mom the world for herself and us kids. She fell for it and then convinced Chris and I that if we all move into his office it will be temporarily cause her new man is going to buy us a huge house with a pool. We fell for it and all move into this man's office near the Yankee Stadium. This place looked pretty well outside but was small and had a rat problem.

I was so embarrassed living in an office. Once, a fellow classmate from my new school offered to walk me home. I made every excuse in the world to avoid this. Out of control, another classmate caught me coming out from under the gate as I was rolling it down. While living here I witnessed a man attempt to commit suicide by throwing himself off a five-story building while I walked from my cousin building down the street. Another time, I witnessed a cab drive get shot by someone in another vehicle and the cab driver slammed into the wall of the Chinese restaurant I was just about to walk into.

Months had past by since Chris last saw his girlfriend and he was not taking it well. Chris would listen to this song by BB and CC Winans that reminded him of his girl. In order to have an excuse to have to see his girl, Chris planned a stunt move. This stunt move was so dumb- Chris threw himself from a storage unit above the office (near the ceiling of the lobby area). The ambulance was called and he was rushed to the hospital. All he kept asking for was " Call my girl! Call my girl!" tell her mother it's an emergency and I need to speak to her". His planned worked because it brought these two lovebirds back together.

My sister Penelope aka Pina ended up moving out with her baby's daddy to Beach Street in the Bronx. My mother and I ended up moving in with Pina and her man. As it got closer and closer to the birth of my first niece. I was so excited become an aunt. I remember I saved some change and bought my sister a bobo (Pacifier) and a nail clipper for the baby. My sister went into labor on November 25, 1988 as she lay on a bare wooden floor. When my niece Heather was born I was so proud as if I gave birth. Pina ended up moving out with her new family and my mom and I stood with the apartment.

Now, that it was only my mom and I living here-came more drama. My mom started making more druggie friends and spending more time in the bathroom. We had no furniture. I remember coming home one evening and my brother answered the door with a black female standing behind him wearing just a blanket wrapped around them. He told me to go —I was confused it was already night time- where else am I supposed to go. Another time my brother stashed some drugs in the house he was selling at our crib- he became hostile after he couldn't find it where he left it. He accused my mom of stealing it. In a panic, he stressed to her that he could get in serious trouble or get killed over this. She quickly denied the accusations and also said I don't care. During the heat of the argument Chris said he was leaving and my mom said go. So Chris left for a few months even I didn't see him.

Now around the age of nine, I moved with my mother to a shelter in China Town. She was trying to go threw the necessary steps to get assistance for housing for us. We stood here for a few days and were given three meals a day here. Once a week all the large departments stores would donate clothing to us (families in shelter) and we all picked out clothes out of the bunch. At the shelter we had to check in and out by a certain time- so I spent most of these days walking the streets of China Town. I actually enjoyed this part, especially at night when the streets lighted up-it looked so beautiful.

Eventually my father came around and gave me a surprise visit at school- he was outside with my picture asking all the kids do they know me. He took me to live with his father on Parsley aver near Park Chester in the Bronx. Here I was bored out of my mind. My grandfather and his seventeen years younger wife were both Jehovah's witnesses. My grandfather was an Elder at his Kingdom Hall and highly involved in his church. We did door to door visits (and you already know how that goes) to drop off watchtowers and schedule bible studies. We spent a lot of time doing this or at the kingdom hall two to three days a week.

Although I am Puerto-Rican/African from my dad and Puerto Rican/ Russian/Italian/Indian/Jamaican from my mom, my Spanish wasn't all that great. The services at the Kingdom Hall were all in Spanish. I remember I was so bored here that I would start cracking up for no reason and interrupt service as my grandpa was on the podium preaching lies. I sucked on my step grandmothers lemon drops just for something to do and made lots of potty trips just to waste time. Besides being overindulged with Jehovah at his home. All I was allowed to watch on TV were "The Sound of Music" by Julie Andrews on VHS or the birth of Sea World's "Shamu" that my grandfather recorded.

When, my dad came around I told him that I hated living here and he took me out. I went back home with my mom for a little then my dad took me this time to live with my paternal

Aunt Marta on Theriot Avenue in the Bronx. During this time, I took turns living with Aunt

Marta and her daughter Yvette who lived in the same building with her husband and two kids. It was this aunt who first taught me how to be a young lady, be clean, smell good (perfumes and such), etc. She took me shopping at Macy's and gave me my first ever perfume called "Coffee"- I treated this fragrance as if it were gold-I made sure to make it last and was disappointed when I ran out. She also told me I must clean my belly button. When I first came to live with her I was dirty looking, smelly, my clothes were filthy, my hair looked like a knotted up dogs hair when not groomed.

During this time my mother would make sporadic visits to see me. Aunt Marta and Yvette were uncomfortable when she came around because they did not trust her. They felt they had to hide everything and watch her every move to make sure she didn't steal anything. The main issue too was every time my mom came around she would ask me for money to support her

habit.

While I lived here my mom moved down the street with a man named "Portfolio" who was the Super (landlord) of a building. She lived with him in the basement of his building.

Around this time, my grandpa and his wife called BCW (children's services) and reported that I was being neglected. A social worker came to see me at my school by the name of Mrs. Walker. She made sure to build my trust and promised to not take my mommy from me. So because I trusted her I told her everything about my mom. My aunt was given temporary custody of me and later a court date was scheduled to decide the best interest of the child- ME. Months later, my aunt received a letter to report to family court with me. On court day my social worker Mrs. Walker was present. Besides Aunt Marta and I, my parents and my grandfather arrived with his wife. My dad just got out of Jail for doing a year for what he says was cause of a gun possession. The tension in the room was so thick that you could cut a knife right thru it. They all were their for a chance to have me-for the first time I really felt like I mattered and cared about.

Before seeing the judge, our case was delayed till after lunch break. My parents asked my caseworker if they can spend lunch with me-and they were granted approval. My parents spent the whole lunch hour coaching me on what to say when I retumed back to the Family Court. My mom said for me to say I lied about everything because I wanted her to get an apartment faster. They told me I could be put in a foster home never to see family again.

In fear of loosing my family, when I returned I did just that. I told my worker it was all a lie. My caseworker Mrs. Walker was furious-she gave me the meanest disappointed look. My grandparents and my aunt were upset as well. My grandparents basically cut me off after that and my aunt seemed disgusted with the whole ordeal. On the other hand, my aunt new that this was not really coming from that and me my parents had something to do with this. I was given back to my mother and she took me to live with her and the Super "Portfolio basement apartment.

My mother often left me unattended with this strange man-thank god he never violated me but it was neglect on her part to do so. At the same time, I was afraid so I remember spending lots of time in the locked in the room dancing cause I was afraid to come out. I remember dancing in the mirror to Rob Base "I wanna Rock" and that song "Doing The Butt" hahahahyup just shaking my thang. Little Suzie was popular at the time. I continued to go to same Public School Aunt Marta had me in.

One day as I played double Dutch on the playground of my school, my brother appeared out of nowhere. I ran to him and jumped on top of him-he said he was in Job Corps all these months. I bragged to my little friends this is my big brother Chris —I was always showing him off cause he was so handsome. When I was a small child I would call him my "butter" cause I couldn't pronounce "brother". I always showed off my sister too cause she was so beautiful.

One day Bronx Children and Families (BCW) came to my school again- my name was called on the intercom again to go to the office- when I turned the comer from the staircase, I saw a person dressed in professional attire that looked to me like another social worker in the window of the office. This time I ran out the back door and my chubby self had some speed. I then jumped a locked gate on the playground and got stuck at the top when my clothes got caught to the metal edges.

This led me straight to my mom's house she shared with Portfolio I don't know how the hell I did it but my adrenaline was running and I did. One day my mom hadn't been home all day so I went looking for her at our old building on Beach Street. I found her at the apartment of this gay older male heavy on drugs and dieing from aids. Here is when her other "get high" part-ner a African American woman threatened to beat me with a bat she picked up from against the wall if I ever were to get smart with my mother again. Truth was I wasn't getting smart, but she was so high she was hearing things.

Another time I was locked out so I walked to Aunt Marta house several blocks over. I had to pee really bad so I went on my self in her lobby. I was so embarrassed but again I was getting even more and more resentful towards my mom and dad because they should be responsible. My mom should be home watching me a child and not have me walking the dangerous streets hours at a time because she was so selfish to be out getting high.

The landlord who let my mom and I live with him ended up getting a new building to watch over at 1079 Hall Place in the Bronx. It was located right beside the garbage dump that attracted lots of mice and rats. The build-ing was such a dump and old that to me it appeared to look a little slanted as if it had a lean. I started going now to another school called "Fox Elementary" down the street from Fort Apache a well respected boxing gym my brother spent a lot of time at and trained with MOE. I ended up moving and going to Fox Elementary School.

Now I was at a new school and had to make new friends all over again. Besides previously being put down as a kid because of my weight, I was now down for my weight and hygiene.

My mother later developed a problem causing her to neglect her role as a parent. Making sure I had soap to bathe was not priority on her list. The crazy thing was that I bathed everyday — but sometimes their was no soap but I tried my best to keep clean using only water, dish soap and even a lemon to scrub my knees and elbows.

At home I quickly became friends with "Margaret Santiago". Margaret was like four years older than me. We lived across from each other on our floor. She was one of eight children (I think). Her family "The Santiago's" became like a second family to me. I felt safe with Margaret Cause she was a tough chick and I was a softee at the time. Matter a fact, I became her biggest fan when I witnessed her get into a planned out fight with "Jennifer" our friend "Stanley" sister at the park down the block from where we lived. These girls boxed like dudes, she looked like Laila Ali out there. No scratching, biting or hair pulling just straight up fists. Often times, I wished I could've brought her to school with me to protect me from some bullies.

There were two tall girls from the projects that were always harassing and tormenting me. They were left back twice, we were in the fifth grade but they should have been in the 7th . I would buy lots of junk food (hot lips, sunflower seeds, now or laters, Swedish fish, anything) just to get to their good side and get them off my back. It worked until the candy was done then they tormented me some more. Other students did the same during lunchtime in the cafeteria. They would say, "You can't sit here-you fat" It was so hurtful because I was very sensitive.

My own teacher humiliated me once in front of my whole PE class. One day during PE in the gymnasium, all of us kids were sitting in the criss cross applesauce position waiting for ours names to be called for attendance. The coach suddenly pauses and says out loud" what is that smell?" "Which one of you is not wearing deodorant?" Before I could even tell it was I, she pointed to me and sent me to the benches in front of everyone. I was so embarrassed, If she only knew I did bathe, problem was my mom did not buy any bath soap, deodorant, etc. cause she was never home to know what we needed and her drug use made her put her priorities as a mother last.

If that wasn't humiliating enough, I was always last pick during PE because of my weight it was assumed by other students that I was slow and incapable of helping the team win. Normally we had a different sport to play every week and the coach always picked several students to be captain and then those students had to take turn picking members for the team from the rest of us that stood against the wall waiting to be chosen. As the choices got narrowed down I always noticed I was the last one picked. When it got to just me, the last captain to pick had no other choicc than to choose me. They would have a look like "damn-why me"-its funny but sad at the same time. This really made mc feels useless al it hurt every time. That all changcd when the game of the day was kick ball. I kicked that ball so hard that next time they were begging mc to be on the team I was no longer picked last-I proved them wrong.

Through all this I continued to be a straight A and B student and never missed a day of school during this time. Although the constant bullying at school could've been a major distraction for some, I continued to stay focused in my work. Academically, school was the only place I felt in control of myself. I knew early on that completing my education would eventually pay off and be my ticket to a brighter future (at least I believed then).

When the teacher and parent day came, I never even told my mom cause I was embarrassed of her and for her. One day when I walked out of school, my dad showed up to surprise me after almost a year of me last seeing him. He was walking around the outside of my school with a picture of me asking children "do you know this girl? Have you seen her around?"

He would sit outside with his truck and honk to catch my attention. On this specific day, he began to cry when he saw me. He asked me "why did your mom send you to school this way?

He said it hurt him to see me dirty, my hair a mess and my purple coat was filthy.

As cheap as he was, I was surprised when he offered to take me to buy a new coat. He ended up buying me a coat, a pair of jeans, Lotto sneakers (with the Velcro colored switch out logos) and brown fake snake leather shoes from Buster Browns. He took me home proud as if this day made up for all the time he wasn't around. Truth was, I had more respect for my mom because bad or good she tried her best and never walked away for good. This was the last time I seen my dad until almost five years later.

I turned ten years old and since my mom was hardly ever around cause she was out getting high, Chris was forced to step up and play the mommy and daddy rolc for me. He made sure I was safe (while he was around) made sure I was in the house by 7pm and not playing with boys. No boys like me anyway because I was even heavier in weight now up to 155lbs. I now was wearing a size 15/16 women's pants at the age of ten and eleven.

I remember playing catch and kiss with friends from my building and block. It was me, Margaret, her brother and some friends. When it was my turn to be it, I purposely ran slowly so the boys could catch me so I can steal me a kiss. When her brother James hid in a closet and I found him I tried to steal my kiss but he was not having it -he mooshed me away and did every-thing possible to keep this chubby girl from landing one on him.

While we outside playing, we see my mother running up the block towards our building. When I look behind her I saw a rat chasing her right into our building-it was hilarious. Our mom would start to disappear longer periods of time now. Now she graduated up to going four days M.I.A. She would say, "Ill be right back or I am going to the store" and come back days later. One time she was gone about two days and when she retumed Chris happen to already be outside chillin. My brother questioned her by asking, "where you been"? What am I supposed to do with Nicky?" "You the mother not me" and she became defensive and said something like " Don't question me! ! !" my brother felt he was deserving of explanation since he was the one left doing her job-I agree. My brother said, "Nicky is hungry" (he didn't even say "we hungry"- his main concern was that I ate). My mom tells him "here" as she past some money to his hands she also says, "I was out getting money for you guys".

As my mom reached her hand out to pass the money to him, Chris yanked it out her hands ripped it up and threw it over the top of a business roof located in front of our building. Frustrated yelling and almost in tears he tells my mom, "we don't want your money we want a mom, I'm not Nicky's mother-you are". They continued to go back and forth arguing and eventually continued the confrontation upstairs in our apartment.

When it all calm down, Chris said he was hungry and for me to make something for him- the problem was there was nothing to make. I looked around and was able to find some left over frozen chicken, peanut butter, hot sauce and some rice. I worked my magic and whipped up the most disgusting meal ever.

As soon as I started to cook my brother and mom started arguing again. My mom came to the kitchen and tried to throw herself out the window. I was screaming "No, No ma" as Chris held her from jumping. She fought for a moment to get loose of him and said, "What do you kids want from me???" "I can't take it anymore". Then Chris let's her go and says" Go ahead! You want to jumpthen jump". As she starting to put one leg out the window she must have taken a good look at that fall to the concrete cause she sure changed her mind- Thank GOD she

didn't.

Finally when everything calmed down for the second time my mom left and Chris asked me is the food ready. The meat was bloody with peanut butter and hot sauce smothered all over it and the rice was hard. Chris didn't care, he said "Give it to me like that"- it was disgusting but he ate it (This was just one of our many cooking stories). Although I was only ten and Chris was sixteen, it was like he was my husband and I was his wife because we looked after each other. I made sure to cook for him and he made sure to keep me safe.

We used to cook our pop tarts between the radiator slits, iron our clothes by leaving it under our mattress overnight. We did what we had too to take care of one another. Chris spent a lot of time in the streets or when he was home he watch "Video Music Box" on the "U' channel as he messed with the homemade antenna made out of a hanger and aluminum foil. Or he stayed on his walkman listening to some of hip hops legends: Slick Rick, Big Daddy Cane, Raekem or when he was on his chill out mode thinking of his girl or fantasizing about "Vanessa

Williams" he listen to BeBe and CeCe Winans, Al. B sure, Keith Sweat, Troop or Surface. Friends would tell Chris he looked like a Puerto Rican version of Al.B Sure and this made him wanna sing in addition to rapping.

One song that truly made my brother break down and cry all the way till he became a man was "House is Not a Home." This song made him think about what a family meant to him and how much he wanted to have one that he could truly call home-a happy and stable one. I remember one night my mom didn't come home and Chris woke me up like two in the morning and said "Nicky wake up, Lets go find mommy". At that moment, all I had on was my mother's fake silk nightgown as my pajama. As I tried to prepare to change for our adventure, Chris said, "Go like That" I said, "its snowing and imma be cold" he said, "be tuff and stop acting like a pussy lets go".

Barefoot and without a coat only wearing a night gown we both left searching for our mom. We walked in the snow from Intervale Avenue to Kelly Street about fifteen to twenty blocks up. I cried and complained and it made my brother frustrated -I was so cold that I got so numb and didn't feel it anymore. We finally found her in a crack spot. Chris said to mom, "lets go" she said "how you going to bring Nicole outside in the cold like that?"

By this point, my mom was heavy on drugs —she went from marijuana to cocaine to crack/heroine. One time she wanted to get her fix so bad that she locked me in a room in the supers apt. As I peaked thru the crack on the door that was locked with a hook lock, I could see her smoking crack with the same man that will soon violate me. In the room, I could hear the rats in the alley messing with the trash. I cried for them to let me out but they just ignored me. Her responsibilities as a mother were far on her priority list. She went months without paying rent or ConEd (light bill). One day my brother and I were home alone and there was a hard knock at the door. Thank god the door had a police lock. My brother said it was the marshals because they here to throw us out. We run out the window, up the fire escape, straight to the roof and waited till they went away. Now that I think back, I don't believe it was the marshalsI believe they were people looking for my brother for a deal gone bad.

Now I am about to experience something that till this day I struggle with. I strongly blamed my parents for this disruption to my life. One night as she was out getting high-she hadn't been home for about four days. Besides being afraid at home alone, it was about 11pm and I was hungry. Chris hadn't been home in about two days. I left our apartment and walked up to the fifth floor to a neighbor's apartment named Cuchie.

I knew this person because she was my friends aunt and was raising other children whom I often played with. She was raising her own children of hers and the children of her daughter who died from aids. When she answered I told her that I was hungry and that I didn't know where my mom was. She gave me some rice beans and meat then offered for me to stay over. I accepted the offer and slept on the top bunk in the same room all the other children slept in. I

remember waking up throughout the night's cause of the roaches that were crawling all over me.

I then go back to bed to wake up next to strange man who fondled me as I innocently slept. This nasty, perverted man had the nerve to pick me up from my bed and carry me to the floor to lie next to him. As if I were his wife, he held me in his arms and held my crouch and rubbed my vaginal area. As he fell asleep next to me, I took a good look at him and realized he was Ralphy-the same man my mom was getting high with when she had me locked in that room.

How dare he do that to me!!! Who can I tell how can I get out this situation safely??? ? . I slowly removed his hands from between my legs and slowly moved out of his arms afraid. I knew if I made a sound he would hurt me, rape me or strangle me to death. I broke free and ran to my neighbor's room and told her. She woke up her husband and in a yelling voice said "why would you put a grown man in a room full of kids???" This is the main reason till this day I am over protective with my own daughters.

On top of that this woman never told my mom-and I didn't either until I was in my carly 20s. In my 20s while in the heat of an argument with my mom, I told her and she replied by saying "stop looking for pity its not like he had sex with you, you probably deserved it." That really hurt me, I was ten years old so how could I possibly have deserved that- she later apologizes. When it first happened, it became a secret and ended up being just one of those things I hold inside. In fear of them both going to jail for murdering that filthy man, I never told my brother or father. I didn't want to live in guilt for them going to prison on my conscience.

The last straw came when I was about ten and a half, when my mother was gone for about four days and my brother did not know what to do with me. Chris called my mothers mother whom we called Abuela . She told him for us to go to her one bedroom section 8 apartment on 133 street in White Plains Rd. When my brother told me we were going there I was petrified because of all the bad stories my mom had told me about my grandmother. We got there and she fed us a hot meal. The next morning my grandmother called BC W (child services) and reported my mother.

Honestly, my grandmother did not want us out of love or concern for us-she wanted us for three reasons: 1. To get that monthly foster care check for us. To prove to everyone that my mother failed and that she is the hero to pick up the slack. 3. She wanted me as her slave to basically serve her hand and foot. Chris and I hated living with her because she was mean, incentive, cruel, prejudice, you name it- nothing good about her —she was simply evil. One time I went with my Abuela to visit her sister and she asked me to walk three times around the complex and crack an egg on the floor. After that she told me to go to the Soundview Park and bury some concoction she made and put inside of a syrup medicine bottle.

Till this day I have no clue what the purpose of this was- I just knew it was something bad. I never questioned her, I was so afraid of her that I did whatever she wanted me to do. She would have us put an act whenever the social worker came around to check on us. Every time social worker for BC W came to inspect-my Abuela would put on the biggest act-like she was a great grandma. She always made sure Chris and I were both there to agree with her on everything. The worker would always question us in front of Abuela like we would say something bad or the truth about her in front of her.

Abuela would always call me a glutten but she would say it in Spanish. In order to teach me a lesson, she asked me what was my favorite meal. I told her spaghetti, so she made me a huge pot of it. She told me to eat every bit of it so it can make me sick and turn me off from food. I must say it worked cause it did turn me off and I soon began to loose weight.

To Abuela I was her slave or Cinderella the step child and she was my master. All she had me do was clean all day. She would give me Q-tips and have me clean her detailed hand carved wood furniture and bar. Then she would walk at swipe her finger and say, "its not clean enough, start over" as she yelled at me. She was constantly yelling at me, calling me terrible names or smacking me in the face. I was miserable and thanks to her I grew up to have Obsessive Compulsive Disorder with cleanliness and organizing with both my body and my home. My grandmother was evil and heart less and I identified her with both the mother from mommy dearest and the grandmother in Flowers of the attic.

A few months later, my mother came to visit me and looked beat up. Her eyes were black and blue and her lip was busted. Although she wouldn't tell us what happened to her, I assumed the worst. It looked like she may have owed a drug dealer some money and got beat up for it or maybe rape. On top of it all, she looked extremely skinny and weighed about eighty-six pounds.

While living with Abuela, she often performed her rituals at home or would have big Santera parties every April. Sometimes I would hear her in the room chanting and dancing on a bamboo matt chanting to some African music as she puffed on a cigar. I remember an incident where my brother asked her "if you don't like black people why do you have black dolls all over your house (these were the dolls that were part of her religion and they were dressed in white or other clothing with a hair wrap and garnished with colorful beads that all had meaning). I nicknamed my Abuela "Grandma Dearest" because she reminded me of the mother from the movie "Mommy Dearest" with some of the personality from the grandma in Flowers in the Attic.

As soon a he asked her, she got furious and jumped up off her chair and chased him with a pair of scissors. As he quickly limped on one leg away from her because his other was in a cast from a sprain during basketball. Chris fell against the sofa and Abuela hovered over him and said in a screaming voice, "don't you ever question me, Ill stab you with these scissors." He started crying out, "why, why you hitting me?" as she continuously kicked him on his sprain leg. Chris froze up and looked at her like he wanted to knock the shit out of her.

I could tell my brother was miserable just like me but he tried to be a man about it or not be a pussy like he would many of times tells me not to be. Chris spent most of his days listening to his Walkman for beats, vwiting rhymes or talking to himself. He'd act like he was talking to Liza (whom he missed a lot) or he would act like he was in a verbal confrontation and argue with himself. I would just stand there and look at him like he was crazy and laugh. One time my grandmother caught him and said "Chris what are you doing? Who you talking to? This is about the only time she made me laugh, she says to me, "Your brother is loco in the head".

I remember Chris and I would play on my grandmother's stereo in her living room and sing together on the microphone. We would listen and sing Luther Vandross "a house is not a home" (one of Chris favorites that made him tear in the eye) or we listen to new edition "Can

You stand the rain". Chris would sing Johnny Gill part and I would sing Ralph Tresvants part.

Or we would take it back and sing our traditional song "Ebony and Ivory". He would tell me "we going to be like the Jackson's Nicky" I'm going to be famous and everybody is going to love me. This is a phrase I continued to hear throughout the years only to later learn he predicted his own destiny. He new he would be a legend that millions will love and later mourn.

One time, Chris and I walked up the hill to the laudermat to wash clothes. After removing our clothes from the drier, he left a yellow stained sock from his construction timberland boots.

A lady comes to use to drier behind us and says out loud while holding sock in the air" whose sock is this" Chris and I looked at each other like I ain't going to claim that-he said Nicky don't say nothing- we were cracking up.

Just to get out the house and away from Abuela, Chris and I started visiting a Catholic

Church down the street and to get some help from GOD. We went about four consecutive Sundays in a row. No matter where we were, Chris and I found humor in everything. This is why I agree with the notion that "laughing heals all wounds." We would crack up laughing in church because we were bored out of our mind and the music was so solemn and basically corny. I started wanting to come just for the bread and wine. I would grab two or three shots of wine until one day I was disappointed because they put grape juice instead.

Chris couldn't take living with Abuela anymore so Chris left and moved with our Uncle Joe in Miami to better himself. He felt by moving to a new atmosphere with positive influences would help better himself so he can prove to be a good man for is girlfriends parents.

After a few months he came back to New York and moved back in with Abuela and I. After just a few weeks, Chris left again and rather sleep in the streets than deal with another day with Abuela. When he decided to leave again, I cried to Chris "please take me with you" he said, "I would Nicky but I have no place to bring you". He slept at different spots of his friends or on park benches, under highways, etc. . .

When I saw him a couple of months later, he had gotten so skinny. He walked in with an army styled jacket tied with a belt. My grandmother would coach me on what to and not to say to him same, as she later will do with me towards my mom. When my grandmother was way out of sight he made library date with me next day after school. I was so excited to see him I stared at thee clock in class all day- when the 3pm bell rang I jetted out the building and off to meet him at the library. I brought him cookies I took from the lunchroom so he can eat something.

A few weeks later he came back and moved back in with my grandmother and I. A couple of months after that we all moved to Miami, FL. I was around eleven and a half and Chris was almost turning seventeen. At the airport on the way to my uncle Joe house to temporarily live, I went to the bathroom and noticed a red spot on my panties. In a panic I yelled for Chris in the hallway and said "Chris, I got blood on my panties he says" what do you want me to do? Roll up some tissue or something!" Chris was the first one I told I got my period for the first time.

After several months living in Miami Chris and I were miserable. I wanted my mother back and Chris missed his girlfriend. Chris reassured me that we will be happy one day and to just be patient. Chris spent a lot of time on the basketball court or hanging wit my uncle. I spent my days watching all my Children, Oprah Winfrey and Jerry Springer day after day all day.

Oprah was the only person to keep me sane because she was so wholesome and I often took advice on the show as hope for me. Hearing other people's struggles and how they overcame them was very motivational.

One time Abuela wanted me to peel a piece of pumpkin (calabaza) for her so she can put it in her white beans. My way was not good enough so she began to hit me, yell at me and call me names like "stupid and Bo Ba (slow)". Chris came to my defense (AGAIN) and said, "let me help, Ill do it for you Abuela". My brother always came to the rescue during these times; he definitely had his little sisters back. In defense she replied, "mind your damn business, she's going to get it right even if I have to beat it into her." Now paranoid, every time I cut a piece I would shake my hands and tremble in fear she hit or yell at me again.

Little by little this woman was breaking my spirits and putting me into a level of low self worth. Around her, I felt incapable of doing anything right. No matter what I did or how I did it, it was wrong. I found myself a nervous wreck causing me at first to experience anxiety then later sleep walking. Abuela would even wake me up by hitting in me in my sleep till I woke up over something she found I did wrong earlier in the day or week-but I didn't, it just wasn't perfect to please her.

At the age of seventeen Chris moved out for the last time. Abuela and I moved out into her own apartment at Hammocks Place apartments in Kendall in Miami. Abuela began to mistreat me even more and made everyday under her care miserable. She did not allow me to watch anything with black people not even "The Cosby Show." This was the one show that gave me some type of hope on what a family should be. I would often daydream like I was one of the Huckstable children and that Bill and Phylissa were my parents. Then when I heard the sound of Abuelas voice that reminded so much of an evil witch or monster, I snapped out of it and it was back to reality-misery.

She would tell me, "you aint shit like your mother and "you ugly like your father. " She even called me a nigger and told me that I looked like a "Mono" (monkey) like my father the ugliest man she ever seen. One afternoon as she watched TV, she called me from my room to tell me that my real family was "The planet of the apes characters" as she pointed to the sitcom showing on TV at that moment. She constantly reminded me that my sister Pina was her most beautiful granddaughter and not I.

During one Christmas get together at our home we took a family portrait. It was a photo that included Abuela, myself and some others from our immediate family. On a later date after being developed, Abuela sat to view all the pictures from that day. As I saw her looking the photos, I asked could I see them too. She says, "Isn't this a beautiful picture? But one thing is wrong Nicole" I said, "what?" she said "you". She said "look at everybody, you don't look like nobody here-your black" I was so hurt but I found the more and more she hurt me the less I was crying. I started to get disillusioned with life, feeling like I had no purpose here, I felt being born was a mistake-kind of like a lost soul.

Later I learned to toughen up and learn I had to hold my own. My sister moved in with us for a short while and brought along her husband and two kids. My grandmother drove my sister nuts in a different way. She had an overbearing affect over my sister and wanted to control every aspect of her life. Other than that, Pina was her favorite and I guess out of guilt she was financially of help to my sister and her kids. As for me, my foster money was only used on me during holidays or back to school. My grandmother bought me junk and made sure everything for her was of quality (Thomasville furniture, etc.). At that time, I loved my sister dearly but began to resent her for never sticking up for me when she witnessed my grandmothers treatment towards me. I felt she was more concerned about herself.

Abuela would wake me up every Saturday morning by banging on my door like she was a warden or cop. She treated me just like the evil stepmother treated Cinderella. I was there to make money off of (foster care check) and serve her like a water boy. As she sat there in her loveseat reading her paper and eating her stale salad as if she were a queen, I would clean for hours then she would wipe her finger or wipe the creases with a q-tip and say it's not clean enough and tell me start over. She made me such a nervous wreck that I developed the habit of shaking my legs uncontrollably when I sat and began sleep walking at nights. Later in life I was obsessed with keeping my own house clean —I think I would consider myself suffering from undiagnosed OCD with cleaning and keeping order.

Abuela was so cruel that she would even tell me "stop telling people Chris and Pina are your brother sister-they are not! just look at you and look at them! you look nothing like them!" She would make me cry and then put her face in front of mine and mock me. Honestly, I wanted to punch the hell out of her but I was a good kid and didn't. She would make me write horrible letters to my mom while she was in rehab trying to get clean and do right (I hate you mom, you a bitch, I never want to be with you, etc...) She made it obvious everyday that she did not care about me or love me. The only time she was good to me was when people were around.

Now age 12, I was so depressed and I started having racing thoughts during the night as I tossed and turned in my bed. One night, I woke up in the middle of the night fed up and contemplated suicide. I went to the kitchen and took out a large butcher knife and I swung my arms up in the air and when I swung it back down I stopped just in time. When I felt that sharp edge near my belly button I said "hell no, that hurts." I wanted to die but feared pain and going to hell. Furthermore, I tried to hold on to faith and stay optimistic —looking forward to my mom coming out, saving me from here and seeing her have the chance to prove the good mom I knew she could be if she was clean.

I tossed and turned all night while a lot of things crossed my mind. I am not a killer and I wouldn't want taking her life on my conscience. Thank God I was able to not have those terrible kinds of thoughts and think about the consequences. GOD was watching all this woman was putting me through and I had enough faith to know he would see me through this storm. I could've done life in prison for a person who already made me feel like I was doing time. I wanted freedom and happiness and this sure wouldn't have helped.

One thing good I could say was she always had a meal on the table for me. Everything was on a schedule as if I really were in prison. Everyday breakfast was at 7:30am, lunch at noon and dinner at 4pm. On the other hand, I often noticed I would become sick with nausea and diarrhea after eating her meals. To this day I wonder if it were a case of monchousain syndrome or was it simply because Abuela fed me old outdated food. She would buy food on sale in bulk from the markets and we would have food in cabinets that expired months or still serve me cold cuts (luncheon meat) that was so outdated that it was slimy, but she refused to throw it away.

She would hit me for no reason (ex. come from school and she say" you were wearing lipstick," I say "no I didn't" she'd say "you a liar, my dolls told me" (the same dolls she had all over her house, they werc black dressed in clothes and furnished with beads). Another time I came home from sleeping over her friend's house and she told me to wear a swimming cap over my hair when I went swimming. When I got home my grandma asked me "did you wear your swimming cap?" Out of fear, for the first time I did lie and say "yeah" she said "you a liar my dolls to me you didn't" and she hit me with a bat that she kept by the door. By this time, her dolls were really starting to creep me out. I was so miserable that I would stare at walls and sit for hours in the corner of my bedroom floor sitting up with my head down and arms crossed across my knees as I bopped my head while listening to my walkman.

The sounds of Baby face "Ready or Not", MC hammer's "Have You Seen Her", freestyle music like Lynette Melendez "Together Forever" and Cora "Where are you tonight" all entertained my ears. It often caused me to fantasize about how I wishcd my life would be and would daydream that I was famous and on stage performing. Then again, the sound of a hard knock on my bedroom door or yell from Abuela would ruin my dream. The constant stress from my grandmother "Abuela" caused me to suffer from constant headaches and stomach aches to episodes of diarrhea.

My grandmother was so dependent on me that she would call me from the other side of the apartment just to change her channel when all she had to do is lean forward a few inches and change it herself. Sometimes the remote laid right on her armrest but she would still call me to change her channel a dozen times a day. She would make a list of groceries for me to buy then send me back and forth to the store to buy the items individually just to torment me.

During one of these trips back and forth, I almost got kidnapped in the Shopping Center parking lot. I would walk about twenty minutes to and from the store then she would say, "I forgot to write down bread-go back to the store!" Then when I returned she would say, "I forgot coffee-Go back! !" She purposely did this to show her control over me and made it known that I was her servant.

During this time, Chris finally got what he been waiting for back in his life, "his girlfriend." They decided to not care about what her parents felt and be together. Chris was struggling to make ends meet and support her. On top of that she was pregnant to his first child. In desperation he went to our families long time lawyer Dr. Gurtzog asking him for financial help. Little did Chris know he was about to get an answer to his prayers. Dr. Gurtzog asked Chris "where have you and your mother been? I've been looking for you yall for years." Chris said "why", the says

"you won a half million dollars settlement from your mothers lawsuit against the City of New York years ago from your

Besides stress, this was the beginning of my brother out of control weight gain. Chris was so excited, he rushed and married his longtime girl-friend and did his own version of a honeymoon. Chris went shopping, bought himself a huge rope chain, and bought a loaded Porsche then and Ford Taurus with system and all. He bought his new wife lots of clothes, jewelry and just about every color freestyle strap Reebok. Finally he felt like a man, capable of supporting his family. After their first-born baby girl "Amanda was born Chris and his new madc family came to Florida to visit Abuela and I.

I was so excited Chris took me on a $600 clothes shopping spree and bought me LA Gear clothes, Cavaracci jeans and some other clothes. On the way to shop, we rode in his white Ford listening to Keith Sweat's" Makc it last forever" on his banging system. I loved the sound of the bass beating my chest. I enjoyed looking at my brother sceing him happy and smiling as he tried to be smooth and sing the lyrics of Mr. KS to his new bride. Chris was soulfill and would snap his fingers and could tell he was feeling the song and words.

Chris decided to stay to live in Miami and found an apartment at Horizons West in Kendall. Chris asked Abuela now that he has money and a place to live, can I go live with him but she declined. Chris and his wife signed a year lease but after just a few months they decided to move back to NY. Chris was homesick and missed the New York fast paced life. He said Florida wasn't for him and that he is a New Yorker from the BX and is gonna stay true from where he was from.

Few months later, Chris came back down to Miami to see my mom who now was discharged from The Good Samaritan Village Rehab in Upstate, NY. At first everyone was so happy to see each other and Chris looked forward to impressing my mother by taking her shopping and bringing us all to window shop for mansions. It was funny to watch them both take pictures in the mansion as they posed with wine glasses in their hands to make it look like they really lived in it.

Immediately, money became an issue between my mother and brother. My mom wanted some money and Chris said he didn't have it so she flipped on his wife calling her names. Chris said I don't even have money to buy my daughter milk and my mother said something that they held against her till the day he died "I don't give a Fuck" my brother said "what, you don't give a fuck about my daughter?' and my mom said "I don give a fuck that's not my problem. I knew my mother did not mean it, but the drugs really messed up her train of thought.

In retrospect, my mom looked great, healthy, clean and refreshed. Finally, the mom Chris and J always wanted was back, this is all wc wanted. She tried to get herself together and find a job. First she found a job at Sizzler's for a day but after a day dealing with carrying stacks of unsteady dishcs- she quit. Then she landed a job as a financial adviser at a hospital and at second job at Courtesy Ford as a car saleswoman. Eventually the courts awarded my mother back custody and we moved out to our own apartment.

The day I left my grandmothers house, my grandmother gave me the dirtiest look and shrugged me away when I tried to lean over and give her a kiss goodbye.

My self-esteem had been broken by many by this point and the constant put downs from my grandmother was still lurking in my brain causing me to develop deep insecurities and a complex about myself. Thanks to her, most of my life I believed I was ugly, fat and stupid. Furthermore, all the girls in school were getting into boys and developing into beautiful young ladies and I wanted to experience being liked by a boy and feeling beautiful too.

At the age of thirteen I became an undiagnosed anorexic. I would nearly starve myself so I could loose weight and look just as pretty as them other girls in school. I would eat 3 crackers for breakfast it for lunch and dinner maybe an apple. I was a social bulimic meaning I would throw up my food only when I went with family or friends to eat at buffets and just so they wouldn't catch on to my illness I would pig out then go to bathroom and vomit. I was already starting to have faint and dizzy spells and had difficult time concentrating in class.

Suddenly, I became so skinny that my ribs were popping out and my collarbone. No one around me noticed I had a problem only that I must have outgrown the "baby fat." The baggy clothing I wore camouflaged the collar and rib bones that started to peak out of my skin. The turning point came a year later when I self diagnosed myself after watching The Oprah Show. Her topic this day was about others suffering from same illness. I realized I had a serious problem that could kill me and it better explained why I've been feeling the way I been feeling. When I was fourteen and Chris was twenty he moved down with my mother and I.

It was flin having him around because he was hysterically funny and always doing pranks. One time his wife ran down stairs screaming that Chris is foaming at the mouth. My mom and I ran upstairs to the bathroom and saw him limp on the toilet. We all screaming then he says "yall all pussys." He was pranking us to make us believe he over dosed on something.

On a funnier note, one time we had no toilet paper so Chris said, "do you have a yellow pages?" We went ahead and used the pages to wipe ourselves then we made front of the imprint of peoples name, addresses and phone numbers stuck on our butts. Another time Chris asked me to get some ice for him from freezer cause he loved drinking water by the gallons daily and cheNÅing on ice. When I opened the freezer I screamed and jumped because the first thing I saw was a hairy beaver looking furry thing jumping around the freezer- he was cracking up — he had set me up to scare me and put a battery controlled beaver in the freezer.

One night I was supposed to stay over my best friend Kat's house and go to the movies.

Instead, we saw a sign in the shopping center that read "Grand opening tonight Club Skylights Teen Night." Kat and I made our parents believe we were at the movies and instead went to the club and danced the night away. We had so much fun we lost track of time and 4am came really fast. Next thing I know, I'm coming out the club and their goes my brother in a cop car looking for me.

When I got home my mother had all my pictures laid out on the table and was hysterical, then she charged at me and I ran up the stairs. Next minute she follows and throws me back down by my hair but Chris saved me from my mom and caught me before I went all the way down. He said "ma take it easy on her, relax I got this." I think my mom had every cop in town looking for me thinking I was missing. Few months later

Chris moves back to NY

Just a few months after getting on our feet, my mother meets a man named Leo while driving side by side on the highway coming from work. All I remember was her telling me we going to have some company —yeah, company that never left. About two weeks after meeting this man she moved him in with us. I was upset because he was a stranger not only to me but she failed to admit he was a stranger to her to. All my mothers attention was on her new man who brought back old habits.

I felt he was no good and I read right through him. Immediately I started noticing some familiar signs in my mother and became highly suspicious that she may have relapsed. My intuitions were right because he ending up getting my mother back on drugs. After putting in a year and a half in rehab, my mothers relapses worse than she was the first time. How can someone so beautiful and intelligent with so much potential for greatness make the choice to ruin her life again.

In retaliation, I started loosing respect for my mother and acted out by answering back and not listening. I felt if she really cared about me and her family she had a sober chance to make the decision to not take the drug for the first time AGAIN. I made sure to stay away from home with my best friend Kat hanging out, hitch hiking rides from city to city, sneaking out of windows, going to clubs and partying. This was the only thing that made me happy and distracted me away from what really was going on around me.

then soon after my mom and her husband decided to move back to NY too.

A few months later, my mom and her boyfriend decide to move to New York and leave me behind in Florida. When my mom first got there she linked up with my dad to try and hustle some money from my brother. My brother and my father got into a heated fight from what I was told and it escalated to the point my brother pulled out a knife on him and threatened to stab him.

My brother felt disrespected and was accusing my father of abusing him growing up. My father denied the accusations and told Chris, "I was only strict to make a man out of you, and I did love you." My brother later tells me about it and says the only reason he didn't stab my father was because he didn't want me without a father like he was. I was confused because although Chris felt this way about my father, many times he has called him and invited him over to hang out with him. Its like he had a love hate for my father due to resentment of not having his own around.

Because I refused to leave Miami, I stood in Miami with friends of the family for a few months. After the school year was over I decided to go back to the Bronx and join my mom at my brothers house on Gun Hill Rd. I remember my brother was so aggravated with me because I spent the first few weeks crying cause I missed my friends in Miami, Florida. Soon I made friends fast and reunited with old childhood ones. I wanted to hang out with friends, go to house parties, you know be a normal teenage. It bothered my brother a lot because he felt that I was isolating myself as if I thought I was better.

The reality was I didn't want to be around drama or anything depressing anymore. It seemed every time I was around my family it was constant arguing and fighting. Certain things I would witness I didn't agree with and chose to just keep away so I don't end up a victim or witness to anything more than I've seen. For the next almost three years, we all lived together and go through some more drama as usual. It was either my brother and one going at it because they had a love hate relationship. At most times my brother and his wife going through their marital issues.

We moved from here back to Soundview area to a private house on Commonwealth Ave in 1992. It was just in time for the New Year and I was now 14 and was entering the 9th grade. My mother enrolled me at Stevenson High School in the Bronx. I was excited but nervous about coming here because I just left Florida and was afraid I may not fit in anymore. Great thing was many of the students I already new from elementary school and this made it easier to blend back in. Although I was shy, I was one of the well-liked girls from school made lots of friends fast soon blossoming into a social butterfly.

I remember I wanted a job so bad so I can buy myself the nice things all the other kids were wearing at school. One day I went to Freddy's to shop for myself and the boss man came up to me and said, "you got good taste, you want a job. " I replied by saying, "I would but you going to say I'm too young." He then asks me " How old are you?" I said 14" He says "start tomorrow after school" I was so excited. He said he'd pay me $3.86 an hour and at my age that sounded like a lot money. So, in September of 1992 1 started my first under the books job as a sales girl at "Freddy's" a clothing store on Third Ave in the Bronx. I remember I went home excited and proud to tell the news of my first job. Eventually my wardrobe got nice my kicks were crispy and I had so much clothes that I went months without repeating an outfit.

I remember in the tenth grade I got into a verbal argument with two girls that been bothering my best friend. In defense of her, I stepped to one of the girls in the girl's locker room and threw my hands up and told her "lets go, pick on me." We were sent to the office and ask to discuss the dispute in front of the principal, guidance counselor and security officer. Next thing I see, I turned around and saw my brother. Chris showed up with his whole crew. To turn and see him truly reminded me how much he had his little sisters back-I really felt powerful and safe. I don't even know how he found out but he popped out of nowhere like a damn super hero.

The girl said something disrespectful to me so I threw a cartoon of juice at her and the officer started to cuff me. Chris stepped in and said " aint nobody doing shit to my sister, that's my word" with this slick laugh he had. My mother then shows up (all late) and negotiated with the principal to let me go and reminded them I am a good student and do well in my classes and this was my first encounter like this. Not satisfied, Chris was telling the girl to meet me at the park outside of school hours and fight one on one but chick bailed out.

I remember one time I walked to the dining area to put my bubble jacket on that I had hanging on a chair I immediately noticed my cell phone, beeper and $20 was missing from my pocket. I knew it was her husband and

I went straight to my brother and told him. My brother confronts my mother but she becomes defensive and starts to defend her man. Chris told her, "why you always defending men over your kids?" An argument broke out and when my mother charged at him, Chris punched my mom right in her eye and she fell back onto my red futon bed. I felt so bad; my mother walked around for a week with shades on cause her eye was so swollen.

When Leo came home and saw her face, he asked my mother what happened. Later on that evening he confronted Chris about my mom and they get into a heated argument. When he got up in Chris face, Chris pulled out a knife and raised his hand in the air ready to "put it in him." Chris kept telling him "imma kill you" Leo wasn't scare and as he took a deep breathe and tightened up his chest, he tells Chris, " go ahead." Afraid for my brother to do something that would put him in prison for life, my mother and I screamed in the background "don't do it Chris." Finally, everything calmed down and Chris eventually moves out with his wife and two daughters.

Now around the age of fifteen, I started to grow and develop into a young lady curious of the dating scene. I started dating a drug dealer from Cozy Corner in Soundview who went by the street name Critter Makes who all the woman went nuts for. He was Puerto Rican and black with light eyes, soft curly hair and dressed really good. At first I paid him no mind but his frequent passes at me were hard to resist.

Young and Naive I fell for the game, believed he loved me and would never leave me like he said. He said he wanted to marry me at the Apollo when I turned eighteen. After many times hearing my mom looking for me and yelling my name on the street from his bedroom window, I was nearly losing my virginity to him. After finding out he was a much more than just liked by these other girls, I dealt with my first stage of teenage heartache.

I remember one night it was like three in the morning and my mom did not come home. I went walking looking for my mom all over the place. I walked to crack buildings and drug spots . By this point in my life I toughened up during this time, nothing fazed me or scared me on the streets. People on the corners or at these buildings would tell me "I ain't see your mother or give me a spot to check." They be like "little girl you think you tuff, go home before you get hurt! !" and I would say " whatever man, I know my mother is in here."

This still wasn't enough to stop me. I would walk around with a shank, knife or whatever was short held tight in my hands as the long sleeve of my hoodie cover it. I wanted to make sure that if anything were to pop off —I was ready. Thank GOD nothing ever did because a bullet to my head would've way overpowered my little ass knife. Later on that night a friend of mine saw me and offered to come wit me . We had no luck finding her and ended up sleeping in his parents car cause I was locked out.

My mothers husband was a handy man and he was offered the opportunity to move us into a home that needed a lot of work for a cheap rent as long as he fixes all out of his own pocket. This house had no windows, ripped up tile, no appliance and no hot water. You guessed right, he didn't fix anything at all. I remember winter came around and Chris had lent me his electric heater because the house was freezing. During the night, my mother's husband walks into my room and takes it. After shivering myself to the point the cold woke me up, I noticed it was missing. I walked to my mom's room and take it back. Her husband comes right back and attempts to take it again so we get in a verbal confrontation and he threatened to hit me.

Now threatened, I pulled out a large butcher knife I kept under my bed and threatened to stab him in the neck if he didn't get out of my face. Mom comes out and again starts to defend her man over her kid. Instead of stabbing him, I pulled out my can of mace and sprayed them both. As they both stood their screaming cause their eyes were burning I packed up my clothes and bounced in the middle of the night to my home girls house for two weeks.

I went to visit Chris at his other new apartment in the basement of a private house. Me,

Chris, his wife and Cuban Link (Phil back in the day) were watching music videos. It was around 1993 and the singer Joe came on the TV in the video for his new single the new single off his album. Chris was like "watch we going to do a song together one day." This was just another thing he predicted in his short to near future. Just like when we were younger Chris had the biggest crush on Spinderella from Salt and Pepa and swore up and down that he was going to marry her.

When I came back we moved Again to a basement apartment a few blocks down on Leland Avenue until they finally broke up- my mother and I had to go to a shelter again- My mom said it was necessary to get a housing apartment fast. Now 1 6, I was to embarrassed so after one night there in Brooklyn I left and told my mother I can't do this. My mom and me move into a shelter located in Brooklyn- this was necessary for my mother to get accepted faster for housing assistance. First we had to go up to third avenue to this holding spot that we waited for hours from like 7pm to the middle of the nightthen a bus transported us to the shelter where we lived for a few days we move to St. Lawrence.

My mom and I ended up moving alone to a private house basement apartment on St.

Lawrence Avenue. it was her she took Leo back for a short while before he left for good — Before that my sister came to visit us on her last day in NY and I asked can I go back to Miami wit her for vacation (my intention was to stay) I left for two months and got a job at Ruby Tuesday at the Dadeland mall as a hostess for two days- The other waiter were getting mad at me for seating people in areas that were closed and had no servers —customers were waiting like an hour —I got tired of them yelling at me and I said "Fuck you —I quit"-

This same summer of 1993 in Miami, I was sharing some pictures with my best friend Kat. I came across a picture with a young man named Samuel JnBaptiste in it. My friend asked me who he was and I told her he was some guy from school that's had a huge crush on me.

Although I was a few months from turning sixteen, just broke up with my boyfriend and was mad at the world over it-I finally noticed him. When I returned to NY that summer, I decided to accept his invitation to be his girl and began dating. We both thought we were grovm and started a young puppy love relationship. Little did I know, he would end up sticking around for a long time?

My mom and me moved again with Chris and his family to a building in Westchester Square. In order to make some more side money to support his family, Chris got a job working the graveyard shift as a doorman for a hotel in Manhattan. I remember it was a cold winter and snowing hard. Although Chris would go to work and back with no jacket he made sure his wife and kids had one. He was a good man with a good heart who sacrificed for others even when he didn't have. Yes, he wasn't perfect- but who is???? No one. After like two weeks of falling asleep at work, he was like "fuck that, working for someone else ain't for me" and quit. This is when I really saw him "Go In" and put lots of hard work, hours away from home to be in the studio and work on his dream to become a hip hop legend.

Around the early 90s Chris went by the name Big Moon Dawg. The full of Clips Crew was formed and included my brother, Triple Seis and Phil a.k.a Lyrical Assassin at the time. They became well known underground in the South Bronx. Each member of the crew had something to offer-Chris now Big Moon Dawg was known on the streets for his lyrical flow that included rhyming at high speeds and tongue twisting his words that ended with a crazy punch lines. Phil a.k.a Lyrical Assassin could rap about being a Latin thug from the hood to a pretty boy rapping for and about the ladies and then their was Triple Seis another great talent from the crew with a crazy flow.

Chris had Juman make him his official "Moon Dawg" jacket. Full of Clips had tshirts made, they did some shows-Chris spent all of his days at the studio at his mans house- he would get mad at me because he would always ask me to stay with him at the studio but I was always to busy being a teenager. even though he definitely had what it took to be a star, I Truely didn't think he was going to pop off. Every dude in NY was trying to be future rappers- so I didn't take him serious.

My brother got really upset one evening when he returned home from work to catch me leaned over one his members "Triple Seis" in the bathroom. Although it didn't look right in his eyes, Triple Seis had simply asked can I wash his hair for him. My brother turned red and flipped on Seis asking him what he is doing. He said something like "what you doing? why you having my sister wash your hair? He threatened Seis to never do some shit like that again or else. At the moment I felt my brother over reacted but I do understand he just didn't want any one of his boys to be funny and disrespect me in any kind of way.

It was this apartment that Chris and Felix aka Cuban Link took me to a modeling audition in Broadway. A big modeling search was announced on the radio that was to be held at a hotel ballroom in Broadway Chris and Phil a.k.a Cuban Link really thought I would be great and encouraged me to audition. They both told me they would take me personally and wait with me although insecure, they convinced me and reassured me that they have my back and believed in me. In the lobby, I stared at all the beautiful woman who were there to model different areas like their whole body, feet, hands or etc...

After several hours and 100s of beautiful girls later, my name was called. Nervous and shy I stood on the pedestal and the talent agent/recruiters stared at me and had me spin in a circle. They asked me for my portfolio but all I had was two school pictures. They ended up giving me a piece of paper and sending me on my way. Well a few weeks later I got that call- the lady said" I was beautiful and they would like me to come back to Broadway to put me with their company —but I turned it down. Dumb mistake- I don't even know really why. This was the second time I shyed away from a great opportunity.

The first time was when I was thirteen and living in Florida, my mother secretly sent in an application and picture of me for me for the miss teen use pageant. I received an acceptance letter to try out and I didn't show up. I just didn't believe in myself enough because this point in my life had shot down peers my self-esteem by both my Abuela and early childhood. Soon after, we all moved again to Mead Street in the Bronx. After just a couple of months, we all get evicted. The landlord complained of too much traffic and the pool table balls hitting the floor in the middle of the night. The actual day the man told us to get out they called cops on my brother. A female officer appeared and my brother made her cry He told her "what you doing here? Get out of here, you think you tough cause you got a heater and the badge?" She started to cry then jumped back into her police car and left. In shock from what I just saw, I was like what kind of cop was that? Chris decided to fight to stay cause he knew by law he has 90 days.

On the day of court we headed to courthouse in a cab driven by Arabic and/or Middle Eastem Man. Chris noticed the driver did not understand English so he decided to mess with him. So Chris started saying to him "your mom sucked my balls last night" and the driver laughing goes "oh yes. " I couldn't help but laugh and we all were cracking u. If the poor man only understood that Chris was straight up disrespecting him. Chris told him "your mom sucks a mean dick" and again the man laughs and goes yeah". I couldn't take it laughing so hard".

When we got out the cab Chris goes to him "tell your mom suck my dick again tonight-ok" and with a smile the driver shook his head up and down and replies, "ok."

Chris was able to live out a few more months here for free. He made sure to stress to his wife not to allow is paternal brother Vincent in his house. My brother did not like him very much nor trust him around his wife. Years later, it turns out my brother intuition was right. Not only should he have worried about his brother but about his own wife too.

Now the age of seventeen, I found out I was pregnant from my high school sweetheart Samuel "Sam" Jnbaptiste. One evening when I was chilling at my brothers house with his wife and Sam I was feeling nauseas. I was so nauseated past few days that my sister in law said, "You sure you ain't pregnant-I said no" so sam and I walked to Jacobi hospital. Dr. runs some test and comes back and says "good new —you going to be a mommy" (Sam is in the lobby). Laughing from nervousness and crying from fear I yell "non no" I came out and told him- looking confused and scared he says "how?"

My first concern was my brother because his opinion was important to me and was my father figure. I was ashamed and depressed that I may have disappointed him. To him I was always the baby sister and it disgusted him if I spoke out of character like curse, or talk dirty cause to him I was innocent. My mother did not even know because she was in a Psyche ward at Jacobi Hospitals West Wing. Even when I finally had the chance to, her mind was so far gone that she didn't really get it.

Same as when I first got my menstrual, Chris was the first person I told I was pregnant. Chris was so upset and disappointed in me that he told me "Get out my face." I felt so ashamed and was upset that I disappointed the one man I looked up to. I ran to my room crying and he followed in soon after and gave me a hug and said "Don't worry, I got you." What a sound of relief that was to hear from him. I had no one else to talk to about it. My mother was in a psych ward at Jacobi Hospital West wing. Her mind was far-gone to understand what just happened.

For the next six months I remained living with Chris then moved in with my Aunt Nora.

Pregnant and no place to stay, I slept squished on my aunts little coach with my big belly until I was seven and half months pregnant. During this time I was able to finish off the remainder of my sophomore year and attend summer school. My whole soon to be graduating class and teacher Mrs. Potter all threw me a surprise baby shower. I applied to Bethune Cookman College in Daytona Beach, FL for nursing and Sam applied for Embry Riddle University in Daytona

Beach for air traffic control. We both were accepted and made plans to move and start school August 1995.

Chris moved to Castle Hill and I ended up moving out right before the shower into my own apartment in the attic of someone's home. Sims parents were strict and didn't want him completely living with me yet so at first he just came over daily. Chris threw me a second baby shower and took this time to question Sam on his plans for us. During the long talk, Sam broke him the news that he wants to move our baby and me to Florida so he can attend college and give us a better life. At first my brother was like "you aunt taking my sister no where," Sam tried to brave up and say, "I love Nicole and I will be good to her." After a few threats and warning to Sam to never hurt me, he gave his wishes and grew respect for him for stepping up and trying to be a good man.

I had a difficult pregnancy because I suffered from hyper-emesis gravidium (extreme vomiting) the entire pregnancy. I lost twenty three pounds throughout my pregnancy. After speaking with my advisor, I learned because of my academic scores as an honor roll student in some classes I could graduate high school early only if I attend summer school. I don't know how I made it threw the summer, I vomited all over the hallways, bathrooms, staircases you name it. In January 1995, I graduated six months early and while holding my diploma in my hand I cried the whole walk home I was so proud of myself because people thought I ruined my life and would not finish school, but I did.

Finally on March 24, 1995 1 gave birth to a beautiful 61b 150z baby girl I named Pascale Monet. She was born sick and had to stay in ICU for ten days. Besides my mom and in laws, Chris was the only person to visit her here. When he saw her in the tiny incubator, he said he couldn't see her like that then broke down in tears and left. I was so overprotective because "she was mine-all mine" now I found that unconditional love I been craving for all my life. Sam little by little started staying more days in a row until he officially moved in. Sam moved in June of 1995 to Daytona Beach, Florida ahead of me to start summer school and look for work to help support us.

I stayed to save money and worked at Robbins on Fordham road then Conway's as a cashier. I moved out and into my mother's new apartment in Academy Gardens until August 1995 when it was my lime to move to Florida for college too. By the time came to move, I managed to save only $600

cash bought a greyhound ticket and off me and my baby went to start a new
.1 had big dreams and high hopes, but all the negativity back home would
have been a distraction. Although my intention was to not be a product of
my environment, I later learn that most of us are.

During this same time, Chris met another Puerto Rican rapper from
the Bronx named Fat

Joe. My brother purposely wanted Fat Joe to notice him so he stood in
front of the bodega Fat Joes was in and was having freestyle battle with his
Full of Clips crew. After hearing him and having him recite, Fat Joe knew he
was one of the great ones and decided to work with Chris.

Chris made his commercial debut on Joe's second album, "Jealous
Ones Envy", in addition to appearing on a b-side to Joe's "Envy" single, "Fire
Water." Chris later changed his name to Big Punisher a.k.a Big Pun, after the
Marvel Comics superhero.

When I first moved it was hard keeping up with Chris because I was
busy with school and he was busy working on becoming a legend.

I was really struggling when I first moved to Florida and had no car so
I walked everywhere. It was so hot and I walked to school and from, baby's
daycare, the store, etc. One time while walking to Kmart with my baby in
carriage, two men followed me in a royal blue tinted Chevy looking car. As I
kept crossing the street back and forth to see if I was being followed, I noticed
then kept making u-turns to keep up with me. I got scared d ran towards Halifax Hospital until I hit a dead end. These two men (one black and one white)
get out the car and start walking towards me saying "hey you." An angel came
this day because a car came out of nowhere and started honking for them to
move their car. This gave me a chance to get away and they drove off.

After several conversations with my mom back home in the Bronx, she
convinced me that she wanted to better her life. I believed when someone
wants to change they must make the first step and she did. Determined to help
her, I sent for her and she moved in with me, my fiancee and new baby. Soon
after my mom moves down and I witness how painful withdrawal could be.

She tried to quit cold turkey and was foaming at the mouth and complained of being in pain. Eventually I found myself bringing her to the emergency room but all they could do was medicated her on pain meds-after a while she wanted to go just for that since she had no drugs.

After a few months, she seemed to be doing better and she convinced me that I could leave my 9-month-old baby daughter with her while I went to work. Around lunchtime, I called home to see how all is doing. When no one answered after my several attempts to call, I began to panic. I asked my boss could I leave because something is not right at home. When I arrived at home I noticed my front door to my apartment was pushed in and the door liner was cracked.

After seeing no one was home, I began to panic and start screaming. A neighbor upstairs yells out, "I have your baby." I get my daughter and tell the neighbor "what are you doing with my baby" she said 'your mom asked me to watch her." She told me my mother was at a mans apartment around the corner of our complex-I banged on that door when a man answers-I tell him "where is my mother?" I then see her before he has a chance to respond-grab her by her hair and yank her out as I tell that man to "stay away from my mom or I will hurt you kill him. He thought he could use my mother and pay her by giving her drugs.

I called the police and had her baker acted and told them she is a threat to herself and others. The police took her and transported her to Halifax hospital. Later on, I went to see her at the hospital and when I asked the nurses at the nurses station where I could find her they pointed to a security TV screen. When I look my mom was on a stretcher tied in a stray jacket screaming. The nurse says to me "is that your mother?? I feel sorry for you. They claim when she arrived she was combative and a threat to staff. I was so embarrassed because I moved to Florida to better my life, go to College but it seem like all I ran from followed me here. How can I ever move on?

During this time my mother was shopping lifting clothes from Kmart then bringing them home as gifts saying she bought it for my daughter (I was like how-you don't have a job) then she would steal the clothes back and sell them for money. Eventually she got caught shoplifting in Kmart and it turned out she had a warrant in Miami for some stolen checks she claimed her ex husband stole from her job at Baptist Hospital and wrote in her name.

After about 6 months locked up and never charged she returns with a new attitude ready to improve herself. She got a job at the Adams Mark Hotel as a pbx operator in Daytona and soon meets her future husband "Naphtali Tirado". She eventually got her own place, and married him. Chris came out with his first single in 1996, "I'm Not a Player" (featuring an O'Jays sample). In 1997, the song's remix, "Still Not a Player"(featuring Joe), became my brother now BIG PUN"S first major mainstream hit. I guess his prediction just five years earlier was on point when he said he would do a song with Joe. That same year Full A Clips became part of Terror Squad. I remember I just got off work at a local fast food spot "checkers" and my brother called me on my way home to tell me to put on the radio. I remember the moment driving way my new ugly purple Chevy cavalier. It was a Friday night and the dj mix came on 102 Jamz and as soon as I heard them announce his name and his new hit song" for the first time on the radio I started screaming out my car "that's my brother, that's my brother" I even almost crashed my car -crying I was so proud and reality finally hit me that my brother was a

star.

No one believed he was my brother, especially on my college campus. People thought I was some obsessed fan. Some people were just so ignorant, they felt if he was my brother I should be the best dressed in school, drive the nicest car, and live in a mansion. I overly expressed the fact that his money is for his family (wife and kids) and I have my own life. On top of that, people think that rappers are ballers but at first they really not, until they sell enough to pay back what was invested in them all that material stuff belongs to the banks still or under the labels name. besides appearing on Fat joe's second album, he also appeared on beatnuts track "off the Books" in 1997. In a998, chris full length debut capital punishment became the first album by a solo

Latino rapper to reach platinum status. this album hit the five spot on the billboard 200 charts going gold then double platinum. My brother had a huge heart and he loved his people and giving back to his community was definitely priority on his

Summer of 1998, chris bought a Mister frostee ice cream truck and had our cousin Weepy run it. He gave free ice cream to all the neighborhood kids and even threw thousands of dollars out the window of his car/limos for people in the street to catch. One day when my mom came down to visit him they went walking around Central Park and he brought a ice cream cone for a homeless man then sat next to him with his arms around him and took a picture together just to make him feel special.

With all this money he threw away to people and neighborhood kids around the way, my mom definitely felt as the mom that she was entitled have some of it too. With her son being a popular rap star, my mom made sure to ask all she can. My mother drove Chris crazy for money and it often led to her telling him degrading things, left crazy messages on the voicemail of his record label. It was kind of like blackmailing because if he didn't give it she would tell him she'd call the label or call peoples magazine and tell everyone how he doesn't support his mother.

From the outside, it looked like a love hate relationship between them but the truth was they loved each other in a dysfunctional way. As much as my mother drove him nuts, my brother liked the fact he was needed, made him feel powerful. My mother loved my brother, he just had her spoiled and it made her greedy. Chris expressed to me often that people think he had a lot of money but he even had to pawn some jewelry just to give my mother money to get off his back. The point was he look forward to supporting her, that was actually something he looked forward to all his life "To take care of his family." He always said he wanted to buy a compound like the "Kennedy's" and have all of us live there.

That same summer of 1998, I came to visit Chris back home him in the Bronx. We stopped at the gas station and some guy tried to kick it to me.

After I tell the I have a man, he says "fuck your man." When I got back to the car my brother said "what did that guy say to you?" When I told him, Chris got out the Benz really quick and upset and walked to the guys car. When he got to the driver window he says to the guy, "Fuck your man? Oh yeah? I'm her man" then he yokes the dude. The guy looked in shock- I'm not sure if its because he got put in his place or because he noticed the man yoking him was Big Pun.

When I returned to Florida, my mother and my family moved into a townhouse together in South Daytona, Florida. It was here that I first saw Chris on the Video Music awards. He was performing with the singer Brandy and Fat Joe. As we all sat in the living room with family and friends, when we all saw him come out we all started screaming from excitement. I became very emotional and was so proud of him. "Look at my big brother" I said to myself, "he did it just like he said he would." Something about him just showed the stage belonged to him, he looked so handsome and confident and at that nothing moment mattered but watching him shine in front of the world.

By this time in his career it was hard for me to visit him often because I was working two jobs and in school pursuing my nursing degree. Chris didn't understand my priorities at the time and told me to quit school and go live with him so he can take care of me. . He didn't understand I couldn't just leave school every time he wanted me near or take off work. My sister Penelope had no priorities holding her down and unlike in the past she was able to make it to NY quite often.

I remember from here I drove to Miami one night to see Chris perform for the first time. The show was "off the chain"; I was so overwhelmed from joy and proud of him. When he walked out on stage and saw everyone's reaction to him is when I knew he was a star. I yelled "1 love you Chris" over and over while the audience showed their admiration toward him. It's crazy, although he came out with Fat Joe-the crowd was going crazy more for him my brother. Few months after that I drove down to Tampa to see him perform again-but this was a little too wild for me. So many groupies and desperate woman just throwing themselves at my brother and "The Terror Squad" members.

Chris came down with Fat Joe and the rest of the Terror Squad to perform at the House of Blues in Downtown Disney in Florida. At first I met up with him at the hotel where I saw him coming down the hallway on a coat cart. He couldn't walk the distance so he had some of his boys roll him around as he held each end of the pole with his arms stretched out. It was getting closer and closer to showtime, but my brother was taking his time and eating. Finally we all head out and are transported by limousine.

When I first arrived, my brother went separately through a back door. I reunited with him in the V.I.P section where Miss Jones stood beside him. As we now stood behind the curtain on stage to get ready for the performance, Fat Joe and my brother say, "Nicky, when we go on stage stay right here and don't follow us on." With a sneaky grin, I say "nah, I'm not.". As my brother got on the mic and hyped up the audience, I was getting hype to as if I'm going to perform to. As soon as Fat Joe and Chris get on stage, my hard headed self comes right behind them. It was so funny to me to see how they both looked at me. My brother looked at me like

"dam, you don't listen" and Fat Joe looked at me with the meanest look. What made it worst was I brought my friend Delores aka DeLo on stage with me and we danced our behinds off. It was such a rush to feel the energy of the crowd going crazy for my brother.

Few months later, I received a strange call from my brother's wife asking to speak to me about something serious. His wife was crying and sounded extremely worried because she got herself into a situation she didn't know how to get out of. She expressed to me that she was cheating on my brother for the past year and a half with the son of the grocery store owner down the block from her mom's house. My sister in law told me she wanted to leave my brother and that the guy was holding her stash of money for her she been saving. She said she was not in love with my brother anymore and she tried to make it work for the kids. She also said she been planning to leave him for a long time and the new guy is not her reason. Besides the new guy, my sister in-law told me her mom has also been holding money for her so that when she leaves, her and the kids are able to get on their feet.

Although, my sister in-law and I had a good relationship at the time, I found it strange that she was telling me something like this. I could have run to my brother and tell him. On the other hand, I wondered if my brother was putting her up to tell me this just to test my loyalty to him. If it was a test, I failed because I never told him or anybody in fear of him hurting himself, her or leaving my niece and nephews without either of their parents over it. Unfortunately, words started spreading around in the streets and it later turned out she really was having an affair and the man mistress was dealt with. This was her first affair but not her last, she hits closer to home later.

Around this time, I get pregnant to my second child, Sabrina Gayle. In October of 1998, I was two months pregnant when we moved to Deland, FL. During December of 1998, Chris came down to visit the family down in Miami and we all met at our sister Pinas house. Chris said he wanted to spend time with me and had me up all night talking and cracking jokes. The next morning Pina made an appointment in advance with a doctor she knows and we all went with Chris to see the doctor. The doctor asked him "do you want to see your kids grow up?" Do you want to be able to do things with them?" he said "yes" and even expressed what was bothering him. He said he would like to fit on the rides again at the amusement parks so he can ride the rides with his kids." The doctor said "if that's what you want you need to start changing your eating habits and start getting in control of yourself or you wont make it to see the millennium." The year of 2000 coming, a day Chris really looked forward to yet feared he might not make it to experience. After this Chris had everybody buying him fruit and other healthy foods but it didn't last long.

When I was about 4 months pregnant I flew down to NY and went to celebrate Chris "platinum Party" at the SONY factory. I remember earlier that day he gave me money to find a hot outfit to wear. When I showed up he looked at me so happy and pleased by what I've chosen and from afar said, "you look dope Nicky." Later on he asked me how much I spent on the outfit? I said "$125", he said you look better than my wife and she spent $6000 on a custom made blue leather pants suit.

Another funny story, February of 1999 1 went with Chris to White Castles in the Bronx after the Sony after party and when we got to the window Chris orders a 24 piece family pack then asks me "order what you want Nicky" I was like "I thought you just ordered for all of us" he was like "nah that's for me"-funny but sad.

This same trip to the Bronx, Chris, Pina, her husband, and One of TS members and I were driving down E. Tremont. Chris and his boy decided they wanted to play a joke on people passing by, by calling people to the car asking for directions then spraying them with the super soaker. At first they got this young guy and sprayed him- he was so mad and in shot. I was laughing so hard until the next victim came along. This was an old lady who looked no younger than seventy. When they sprayed her the woman acted like she got shot, it was so dramatic. I felt sorry for her, I didn't know whether to laugh or cry. The last victims were a couple who wasn't having it so they flagged down a police car.

Next thing you know, we have six cop cars surrounding us telling us all to "get out the vehicle with your hands up." The cop tells my brother "where is the gun?" my brother says, "We don't have a gun it's a supper soaker." They ask again for all of us to get out and when the cop grabbed me my brother says, " be careful with my sister! She is pregnant." Now we all standing by the gate and out of the audience watching, a fan loudly yells "yo, that's PUN." Next minute the cop tells all of us to get back in vehicle and asks my brother "you really PUN? My son is a big fan of you can you sign him a autograph?" Chris signs it and the cop lets us go without a ticket just some friendly advice "don't do that no more." When we drive off Chris says, "Yeah, you see how that cop was on my balls? He ain't do nuzzzzing."

It was now Grammy time in February 1999 and my brother was nominated for a Grammy along with Jay-Z. The family was so excited about this event and the reality that Chris was a star was the all time high for us all. A few days before the Grammy awards I had a horrible dream that all my family was on the plane heading to California for the Grammy's and the plane crashed. Already afraid of planes, this dream made me make a final decision not to go. I shared this dream with my mom and sister but they were like "forget that, I'm going" and they did.

They got there and back safe and sound along with all the stories about how much fun they had.

My brother lost to Jay Z but regardless he was the winner to me.

On March 21, 1999, I gave birth to my second beautiful daughter named Sabrina Gayle. Wow I was so happy and felt so lucky to be blessed with such wonderful children. I flew down to NY when she was a few weeks old to visit Chris. Chris was so happy and held her on his huge chest; she was so small she just took up the right side of his chest.

This was the same time trip Chris played a terrible stunt on me. He had his boy Sunkiss play a joke on me as if he were on the phone with is girl arguing. During the argument he said something similar to "I Love You, I can't take it" then pulled out a heater (gun) and pulled the trigger at his head. As soon as I saw the heater come up from his waist, I screamed and grabbed Chris but he was so huge he wouldn't budge. I said to myself "hell nah, im out" and ran towards the kitchen. All of a sudden I here them both cracking up then I realized it was a joke.

It was down here I noticed my brother was so overweight, he had little ulcers all over his belly, and his legs were as gray as an elephant's trunk and almost as hard as a rock. His wife had to bathe him in the kitchen with a water hose. After a while the tile began to crack and brake from the constant moisture. His toilet was put in the kitchen because the bathroom was too small for him. His bed was in the dinning area and his chair was a black seat taken from a van. He needed a lot of help and although you can tell she preferred not to-his wife catered to him hand and foot.

I also witnessed how my brother made my niece and nephew's spar (box) against each to the point their gloves had blood on them. As I witnessed, to myself it upset me and I didn't approve of it. On the other hand, I understood my brother's positive intention behind it. He was preparing them for the outside world, the "Real World" -the jungle. He wanted them to learn how to protect themselves-or in his words not be a "pussy". I think deep down inside he felt he was going to die and he wanted to make sure they can hold their own when "papi was gone." This was the time when we were left alone and he opened up to me about his wife. he told me, "Nicky you don't know Liza like I do, She is not as innocent as you think." Later I will see he was not lieing and many of their issues were due to his wife's infidelity, sneaking around, hiding money and things he found on his hidden camera. He had his wife believe the cameras in the house were broken and this is how he noticed some things. His wife was spending lots of time with his paternal brother while he was not at home. This is the same brother my brother mentioned in the past he did not want in his home. They were getting very close, smoking weed together and kissing on the sofa.

By 1999, my brother continued to struggle with his weight fluctuating between obesity and morbidly obesity. Around mid 1999,Chris enrolled in a weight loss program in North Carolina. When I came down to visit, he expressed to me how much he wanted to lose weight but it was so hard. The food he had to eat was so disgusting and the serving size wouldn't even fill up my 5-year-old child, After loosing almost one hundred pounds, he quit the program and went back to New York and gain back the weight he lost and more.

It was down here Chris talked me into getting my first tattoo and first piercing on my eyebrow. I remember it hurt and again Chris said "take it like trooper stop being a pussy." Later that day, I went with him to the studio to work on album "Yeah Baby", and his song "Mama." I remembering staring at the mic like "damn", I wish he would ask me "Nicky, let me hear you sing." I wanted so bad to try it but was afraid he wouldn't take me serious or just laugh at me, so I never had the chance to tell him.

We ended up getting into an argument about money and my mother. It all started when it was obvious he was trying to tease me by bragging about some money he gave to a family member. Unlike others whom asked him for money out of greed, I asked him a handle full of times for help with emergency things (pay daycare, light bill, etc..). I made sure I did what I had to do on my own to get by everyday. He just wanted me to get jealous and ask him, but I was very prideful.

My pride really upset him because he felt that I didn't need him. I just don't sweat no one for anything. I told him "that house and that car I can have, it might take me longer, but I can get it on my own. ? On the other hand, deep down inside he respected me for not sweating him for his mommy. He tried so hard to help everybody and told me to be patient because he wants to get mommy set first then our sister Pina because he said without help she wouldn't make it and he knew I would be alright to hold on a little longer because of the career path I was pursuing.

I felt he didn't love me anymore and resented me for something but didn't know what. It started to bring up things that bothered him about me from when I was a kid and a teen, He said he felt resented because I use to chose to hang out with my friends instead of him, I would fall asleep at the movie theaters when all he wanted to do was spend time with me, and when him and his wife were having hard times, instead of offering to buy milk and diapers I would buy myself clothes.

I tried to express to him that I was a kid and didn't know how to think like and adult. He said if I loved him I would've moved to NY, watch what he ate and help him. I explained to him, "I cant just leave, I am married." He said "if your husband don't want to come then just leave him." When it came to arguments, his stubbornness made it impossible for you to speak to him when the issue was about who was right or wrong. Everyone tried to help, but it wasn't a easy job- at the end he had the last say so.

This argument led to him asking me "did your husband ever cheat on you?" I then replied by saying, "before worrying about what is going on in my house you need to worry about what your wife is doing when you not around." I was speaking in reference to her affair with the guy at the bodega in Bronx River and the longtime affair with my brothers paternal brother Vincent. I thought I was the only one who knew about it. His wife looked at me with the most angry face as she sat beside him. In shock that I hinted to my brother that I knew, his wife's jaw dropped straight to the ground as if she was asking herself, "did this girl just put me on blast?".

The last time I seen him he came to Deland, fl to see my mom and me. He came around midnight and begged my mother to bake some homemade macaroni & cheese. He had about three bowls with some pork chops and a few slices of bread with butter. After the late night meal, we all sat down to talk and crack jokes. A lot of laughs later, the morning started to creep around and our conversation led to the topic of my father again. Chris said my father abused him and I asked him, "how ? be more specific" He said I should know but I didn't remember ever witnessing any physical abuse. Nearly in tears and obviously frustrated, Chris never gave me a clear answer. Now, I'm curious so I ask him, "do you mean sexually? and he answered "NO".

He told me to stop playing stupid and why don't I defend him. He says, "why does everyone want to be defended but no one ever does that for me? Truth was, I would have been happy to defend him if I had remembered anything like that. I admit my father was a terrible father, never was their and theirs nothing good to defend him about. Regardless of that, Chris was bothered that I didn't recall it. I told him I believed him when he says he was abused , but

I don't remember actually witnessing. He felt no one understood him, but I did. As much as he wanted understanding, I was living with pain myself.

The problem was we been through most of the same things and had the same needs and wants.

On February 5, 2000, Chris and Fat Joe were scheduled to perform on NBC's "Saturday Night Live", alongside Jennifer Lopez -but he did not appear. On February 7th 2000 around 4: 15pm, I was on my way to work when my mother called my cell phone and said " Chris stop breathing but they brought him back." Normally, I wouldn't believe it because Chris was always playing stupid jokes like that. I choked up and my chest felt tight, I just knew this time was no joke. I flew in my car to my mothers home and as soon as she opened the screen door she screamed "He's gone. " I dropped to my knees near the doorway just screaming till I couldn't scream anymore. I went crazy, broke things, banged my head against the wall. Unexpectedly, my whole world fell apart. My brother was only twenty eight and weighed 698 1bs making him a health risk. On the otherhand, I grew highly suspicious of his actual cause of death.

My first instinct was his wife is not telling us everything. I immediately called his wife and told her, "I know you killed brother." The reason I felt this way was because I remember the talks of her affair, her previously expressing she was unhappy with him and how much she wanted to get away from him but was afraid that would never be possible as long as he is alive. Till this day, I would take a lie detector test to prove her conversation with me-at the same time,

I asked her to take a lie detector test to prove she had NOTHING to do with my brothers death. [For now, this is strictly my opinion and intuition regarding my brothers death and I strongly stick by it]

On February 7, 2000 Chris was staying at the Crowne Plaza Hotel with his wife while renovations were being done on his home in the Bron. Oddly, his wife had sent the kids away for the day. According to his wife version of the story, my brother suddenly had trouble breathing. She called Fat Joe and asked what should she do? According to Fat Joe in an interview, he was shaken up and wondered "She didn't call me to say he was dead." She called everyone but emergency first. She said she did not give him CPR because he had to much foam in his mouth.

My brother was rushed to White Plains NY hospital that Monday after his wife said he collapsed. He was pronounced dead at the hospital at 3:53pm after paramedics could not revive him. The cause was to be determined by the medical examiner, but it appeared he died of a heart attack. On the day of his death, Dr. Louis Roh at the Westchester County Medical Examiner's office performed an autopsy on my brother and concluded that *while further standard tests needed to be performed*, the rapper's death was preliminarily being attributed to heart failure brought about by a weight-related condition known as cardiac hypo trophy, or enlarged heart. Since my brothers wife had him cremated quickly against his wishes, the further testing needed was never performed. Was this the perfect murder?

His funeral was three days long. Fans were lined up for blocks that went around miles of corners. In tears, fans even waited on thc long lines over and over again. When I finally saw him in person reality finally hit me and I went nuts. I yelled at his selfless body, "Why you had to leave me?why?" I love you, I need you, Please come back to me!" I stood by his side and laid over his chest hours at a time. I kissed on the lips and forehead repeatedly (I almost fell asleep on him) I wanted to spend as much time with him for one last time. Besides this is what he would want, time with his family and friends. I whispered in his ear "I'm going to finish it off for you baby, I promise." Unsure of what I meant by that, I wondered would it be with music, accomplish my own goals because he would only want the best for me or telling of this story.

His wife and I stood far from one another at the funeral as a precaution if my brothers wife try to retaliate towards me over my accusations of her killing my brother or having something to do with his death. Till this day, I truly do not feel he died only of natural causes. In my opinion, something other than natural caused him to have a heart attack. Why would his wife have him cremated if he always wanted to be buried next to his father in Queens?

I observed my sister in law showed no signs of a grieving widow. At the funeral, I noticed she looked quite happy as she smiled and had a laugh or too with some of her family and personal friends. Something just wasn't right to me. When the celebrity friends began to arrive, his wife sat in front of his casket like a queen excepting checks from a lot of the celeb friends offering support for the family. Lil Kim was one who gave a donation to the happy widow.

I wanted to die and even stared at an officer's gun on his waist while thinking how to grab it and shoot myself. I thought about throwing myself off the train tracks near the train subway station above the funeral. I just wanted to be with him and the fear of leaving my children without a mother was what prevented me. When it came time to load his casket into the vehicle for transport to cemetery, I jumped in the back with his casket until several men grabbed me and took me out.

At the cemetery only four people allowed in. Originally it was suppose to be my brothers wife, Cuban Link and my sister Pina —one extra person was needed. I became extremely upset with my sister because she offered for her paternal sister Nyree to go as the forth person. I said "I am the one who was raised with Chris and went thru everything with him, how could you have her go?" Chris had no close relationship with this younger sister who just got back into his life after years of being M.I.A. I wasn't having that, I said "hell no I'm going in." So as they all walked down the stairs towards the cremation , I came behind and barged my way in past the guard-nothing was keeping me from going in.

Pina and her paternal sister Nyree ended up staying out and instead Chris kids came in. I was disgusted to see my niece and nephews fight over who will press the button first to start the oven to burn their father. I took it as if the kids wanted to see conformation that their dad was dead. I also feel it was indecent for my brothers wife to allow his children to witness the crema-tion. It bothered me because he was cremated and wont be able to visit him like I would if he had a normal grave sight. Furthermore, I was not satisfied with his wife's decision to have him cremated because he always said he didn't want to be cremated and burned . I felt the cremation was to cover something up or in otherwards destroy evidence but I didn't speak up to anyone about it.

A final autopsy was never completed according to Dr. Roth at the Westchester examiners office. His publicist David Granoff, however, said that it is probable that he suffered a massive heart attack. The cause of death was pending the results of a toxicology test that never was completed. Initially, an autopsy found that my brother' s heart and lungs were seriously damaged by his weight, which had reached 698 pounds. He had an enlarged heart- three times its normal size-caused by his extreme obesity. His lungs showed signs of failure and had begun to fill with fluid, a sign that his heart was working too hard.

This whole time spent between the two funeral services and cremation, I was extremely depressed. I already missed him so much and just wanted to go be with him. As my family stayed in the hotel room to mourn and support each other, I separated my self and walked out to the balcony. As I stood alone outside I thought about throwing myself over. I then threw a pebble over first and when I heard that pop after it hit the concrete I was like "Oh no, I ain't going nowhere" like my brother once said.

Chris's Yeeah Baby was completed before his death but was issued in April 2000 (two months after he died). It peaked at #3 on the Billboard charts and earned Gold record status within three months of its release and later went platinum. His last compilation album, Endangered Species, was released in April 2001. As with his other albums, it also peaked in the top ten of the Billboard 200, reaching #7, but didn't sell as much as the previous Pun albums had.

I learned years later that several weeks before my brother death, the cousin of my sisterin-law who goes by the name of Scorpio shared with my cousin Boobie that he knows different ways to kill someone without evidence and showed him on the computer. Then two weeks before my brother's death, my brother's wife tells Boobie "I don't feel Chris is going to be around much longer." How would she know that???? He's been fat and unhealthy for the longest-why then she knew it would be his time???

Chris wanted so much to be loved and sometimes that need caused him to do anything to keep you near. Although some actions may have not been except able, my brother was a good man with a good heart who would've done anything to help a stranger. Chris had a mischievous sense of humor and was very comedic. He was no animal but just a gentle giant who needed help but never got it. You cannot take a stray wild cat off the street and make it a house pet overnight. Patience, love and nurturing would've eventually calmed it down and make it humble.

After the loss of my only brother, I felt like a lost soul roaming the earth. The

constant reminder of this tragedy over MTV, BET, VHI, the news and papers made it difficult to heal. Walking by superrnarket magazine stands seeing my brother on the front page made it even more difficult. I then went in a moment of denial. It's like a part of me knew he was going to die soon, but another part felt he was to strong to go anywhere and took time for granted. I wanted to die to be with him, if I didn't have to feel pain or go to hell I would've killed myself.

Till this day I struggle with the loss of my brother. Furthermore, not feeling 100% convinced of his cause of death, makes it hard for me to heal. I sometimes feel he speaks through me and at times I feel him crying out through me. I have dreams of him a lot and even feel his spirit around me as if he wants my help so he can finally lay to rest. I strongly believe this story was not of my own doing but that of my brothers. To bad he didn't have the chance to see me finally break the cycle and prove I could "be shit" and better.

Thanks to my brothers inspiration, I went to College as a single mother of two girls while working two jobs. In May of 2005, I kept my promise to my brother to "finish it off" and become the first person in my immediate family to obtain a college degree-a Bachelors of Science in

Healthcare Administration. In December 2021, I obtained my Masters of Science in Clinical Research Organization and Management. Currently in 2022, I am attending my doctoral program to become a Doctor in Health Services.

Now an adult, I understand my mother's drugs use was an escape from the pain she endured during her upbringing. Watching my mother's proud face as she watched me walk on stage to get my first degree was priceless. This was my way of letting her know I forgave her and that good did come out of all this. In addition, seeing my grandmother's "Abuela" face as I walked on stage and then by the aisle near her was the best feeling. I proudly looked at her to let her know that regardless of all the put downs and verbal abuse she gave me, the little girl she once called "nigger" made it.